MORE JAZZ STANDARDS

**MELODY LINE, CHORDS AND LYRICS
FOR KEYBOARD • GUITAR • VOCAL**

HAL•LEONARD®

ISBN-13: 978-1-4234-1120-8
ISBN-10: 1-4234-1120-X

HAL•LEONARD®
CORPORATION
7777 W. BLUEMOUND RD. P.O. BOX 13819 MILWAUKEE, WI 53213

Visit Hal Leonard Online at
www.halleonard.com

Welcome to the PAPERBACK SONGS® SERIES.

Do you play piano, guitar, electronic keyboard, sing or play any instrument for that matter? If so, this handy "pocket tune" book is for you.

The concise, one-line music notation consists of:

MELODY, LYRICS & CHORD SYMBOLS

Whether strumming the chords on guitar, "faking" an arrangement on piano/keyboard or singing the lyrics, these fake book style arrangements can be enjoyed at any experience level – hobbyist to professional.

The musical skills necessary to successfully use this book are minimal. If you play guitar and need some help with chords, a basic chord chart is included at the back of the book.

While playing and singing is the first thing that comes to mind when using this book, it can also serve as a compact, comprehensive reference guide.

However you choose to use this PAPERBACK SONGS® SERIES book, by all means have fun!

CONTENTS

(contents continued)

ACROSS THE ALLEY FROM THE ALAMO

Words and Music by
JOE GREENE

Easy Swing

A - cross the al - ley from the Al - a - mo,_ lived a

pin - to po - ny and a Na - va - jo,_ { Who / Who

sang a sort of In - di - an Hi - de - ho_ to the
used to bake fri - jo - les in corn - meal dough_ for the

peo - ple pass - ing by._ The
peo - ple pass - ing by._ They

pin - to spent his time a - swish - in' flies_ and the
tho't that they would make some eas - y bucks_ if they're

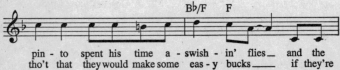

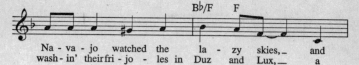

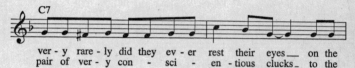

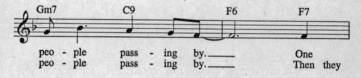

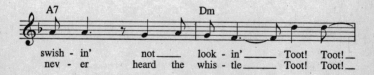

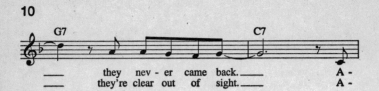

they nev - er came back.____ A -
they're clear out of sight.____ A -

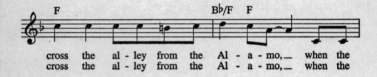

cross the al - ley from the Al - a - mo,__ when the
cross the al - ley from the Al - a - mo,__ when the

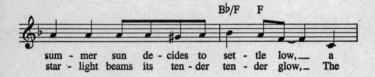

sum - mer sun de - cides to set - tle low,__ a
star - light beams its ten - der ten - der glow,__ The

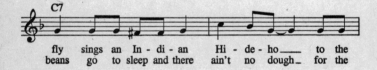

fly sings an In - di - an Hi - de - ho____ to the
beans go to sleep and there ain't no dough__ for the

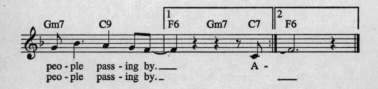

peo - ple pass - ing by.____
peo - ple pass - ing by.__ A -

CHANGE PARTNERS

from the RKO Radio Motion Picture CAREFREE
Words and Music by
IRVING BERLIN

Slowly

Must you dance ____ ev-'ry dance ____

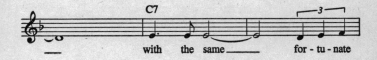

____ with the same ____ for - tu - nate

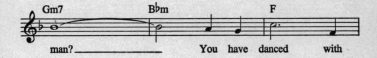

man? ____ You have danced with

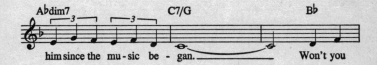

him since the mu - sic be - gan. ____ Won't you

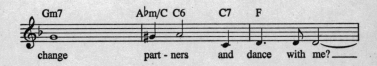

change part - ners and dance with me? ____

I'll tell the wait-er to tell him he's want-ed on the

tel - e-phone. You've been locked_____

in his arms_____ ev - er since_____

_____ heav-en knows when._____ Won't you

change part-ners, and then_____ you may

nev-er want_ to change_ part-ners a - gain.

gain._____

ALL OF ME

**Words and Music by SEYMOUR SIMONS
and GERALD MARKS**

them. Your good - bye left me with eyes that cry, How can I go on, dear, with - out you? You took the part that once was my heart, So why not take all of me? me?

ALL OR NOTHING AT ALL

Words by JACK LAWRENCE
Music by ARTHUR ALTMAN

Moderately

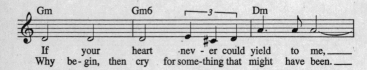

All _____ or noth-ing at all!
All _____ or noth-ing at all!

Half a love nev-er ap pealed to me.
If it's love, there is no in be-tween. _____

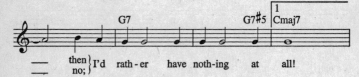

If your heart nev-er could yield to me, _____
Why be-gin, then cry for some-thing that might have been. _____

— then } I'd rath-er have noth-ing at all!
— no; }

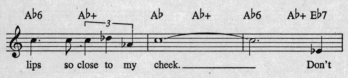

all. _____ But, please, don't bring your

lips so close to my cheek. _____ Don't

ALL THE WAY

from THE JOKER IS WILD

Words by SAMMY CAHN
Music by JAMES VAN HEUSEN

When some - bod - y loves you, it's no
When some - bod - y needs you, it's no

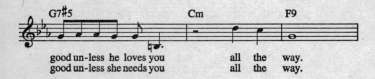

good un-less he loves you all the way.
good un-less she needs you all the way.

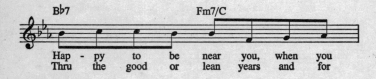

Hap - py to be near you, when you
Thru the good or lean years and for

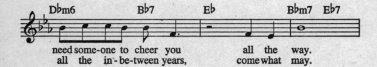

need some-one to cheer you all the way.
all the in - be-tween years, come what may.

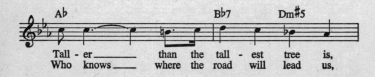

Tall - er _____ than the tall - est tree is,
Who knows _____ where the road will lead us,

G7

Cm Bbm7 Eb7b5

that's how it's got to feel.
on-ly a fool would

Ab Bb7 Bdim

Deep-er_____ than the deep blue sea is,

Cm F7 Fm7b5 Bb7

that's how deep it goes,__ if it's real.

Cm Abm6 Cb Eb

say. But if you let me love you, it's for

Db9 C7 Am7b5 Fm6/Ab Gm7b5 C7

sure I'm gon-na love you all the way,

Fm7b5 Bb7b5 Eb Db9 Eb6/9

all the way._____

AREN'T YOU GLAD YOU'RE YOU

Words by JOHNNY BURKE
Music by JIMMY VAN HEUSEN

Ev-'ry time you're near a rose, aren't you glad you've got a nose? And if the dawn is fresh with dew, aren't you glad you're you? When a mead-ow-lark ap-pears, aren't you glad you've got two ears? And if your heart is sing-ing, too,

BASIN STREET BLUES

Words and Music by
SPENCER WILLIAMS

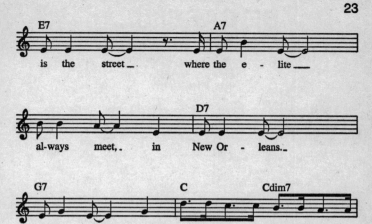

is the street ___ . where the e - lite ___

al-ways meet, . in New Or - leans. ___

Land of dreams, ___ you'll nev - er know, how nice it seems, or

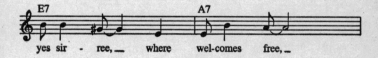

just how much it real - ly means. Glad to be, ___

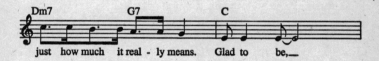

yes sir - ree, ___ where wel-comes free, ___

dear to me. ___ Where I can lose, ___

my Ba - sin Street Blues. ___

BE CAREFUL, IT'S MY HEART

from HOLIDAY INN

Words and Music by
IRVING BERLIN

— it's my heart._____ The

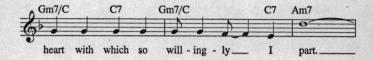

heart with which so will - ing - ly___ I part.___

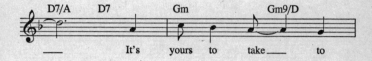

— It's yours to take___ to

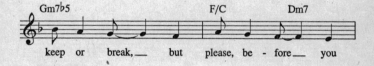

keep or break,___ but please, be - fore___ you

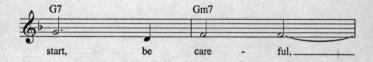

start, be care - ful,_____

— it's my heart.___ Be

BEAT ME DADDY,
EIGHT TO THE BAR

Words and Music by DON RAYE,
HUGHIE PRINCE and ELEANOR SHEEHY

Medium Boogie Woogie

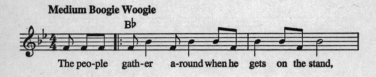

The peo-ple gath-er a-round when he gets on the stand,

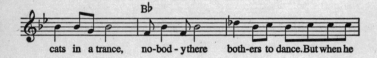

then when he plays he gets a hand. The rhy-thm he beats puts the

cats in a trance, no-bod-y there both-ers to dance. But when he

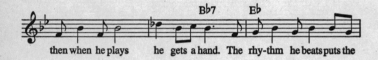

jams with the bass and gui-tar,___ they hol-ler "Aw

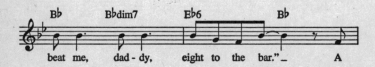

beat me, dad-dy, eight to the bar." _ A

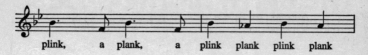

plink, a plank, a plink plank plink plank

plunk-in' on the keys, _____ a riff, a raff, a

riff raff riff raff riff - in' out with ease. _____

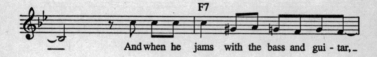

_____ And when he jams with the bass and gui - tar, _____

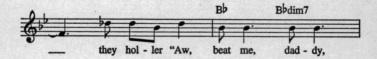

_____ they hol - ler "Aw, beat me, dad - dy,

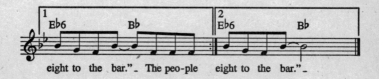

eight to the bar." _ The peo-ple eight to the bar." _

THE BIRTH OF THE BLUES

from GEORGE WHITE'S SCANDALS OF 1926

Words by B.G. DeSYLVA and LEW BROWN
Music by RAY HENDERSON

Tempo di Blues

— note._____ Pushed it through a

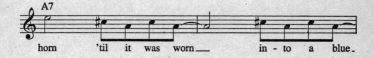

horn 'til it was worn__ in - to a blue

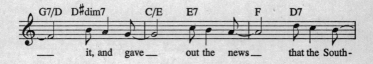

— note!_____ And then they nursed it, re - hearsed

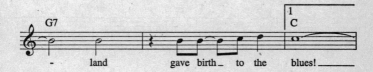

— it, and gave__ out the news__ that the South-

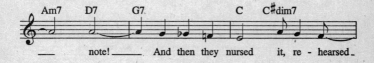

- land gave birth__ to the blues!_____

— They heard the blues!_____

BUT BEAUTIFUL

from ROAD TO RIO

Words by JOHNNY BURKE
Music by JIMMY VAN HEUSEN

Love is tear - ful or it's

gay; It's a prob - lem or it's

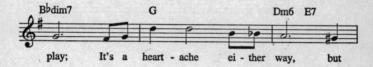

play; It's a heart - ache ei - ther way, but

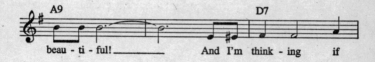

beau - ti - ful! And I'm think - ing if

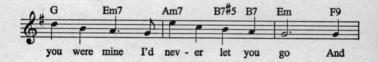

you were mine I'd nev - er let you go And

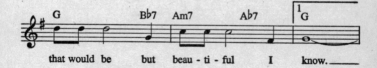

that would be but beau - ti - ful I know.

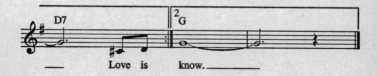

Love is know.

CANDY

Words and Music by ALEX KRAMER,
JOAN WHITNEY and MACK DAVID

CHEEK TO CHEEK

from the RKO Radio Motion Picture TOP HAT

Words and Music by
IRVING BERLIN

COME FLY WITH ME

Words by SAMMY CAHN
Music by JAMES VAN HEUSEN

Moderately slow

When Dad and Moth - er dis - cov - ered one an -

oth - er, they dreamed of the day when they

would love and hon - or and o - bey,

and dur - ing all their mod - est spoon - ing,

they'd blush and speak of hon - ey - moon - ing.

And if your mem - o - ry re - calls,

they spoke of Ni - ag - 'ra Falls____

____ But to - day, my dar - ling, to -

day, when you meet the one you

Moderately, with a strong beat

love, you say:____ Come

fly with me!__ Let's fly!____ Let's fly__ a - way!__

____ If you can use__ some ex -

ot - ic booze,__ there's a bar in far Bom -
(views,) __

bay.   Come   fly   with   me!__   Let's   fly!__

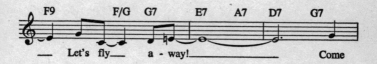

__   Let's fly__   a - way!_____   Come

fly   with   me!__   Let's float__   down to__   Pe - ru!__

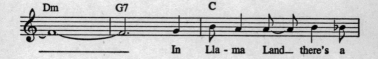

_____   In   Lla - ma   Land__ there's   a

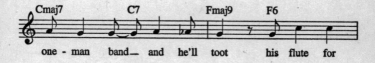

one - man   band__ and   he'll   toot   his   flute   for

you.   Come   fly   with   me!__   Let's   take__

__   off in__   the blue!__   Once   I   get   you

40

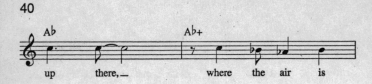

up there,— where the air is

rar - i - fied,———

we'll just glide,— star - ry - eyed.—

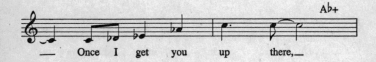

— Once I get you up there,—

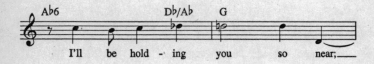

I'll be hold - ing you so near;—

— you may hear———

an - gels cheer 'cause—— we're to - geth - er.

DO NOTHIN' TILL YOU HEAR FROM ME

Words and Music by DUKE ELLINGTON and BOB RUSSELL

DON'T BLAME ME

Words by DOROTHY FIELDS
Music by JIMMY McHUGH

EASY LIVING

Theme from the Paramount Picture EASY LIVING
Words and Music by LEO ROBIN
and RALPH RAINGER

⁴⁶DON'T WORRY 'BOUT ME

from COTTON CLUB PARADE

Lyric by TED KOEHLER
Music by RUBE BLOOM

Moderately

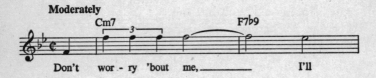

Don't wor - ry 'bout me, _____ I'll

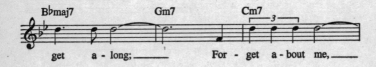

get a - long; _____ For - get a - bout me, _____

__ be hap - py, my love. _____ Let's say that

our lit - tle show is o - ver and so, the sto - ry ends; _____

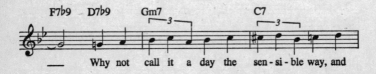

__ Why not call it a day the sen - si - ble way, and

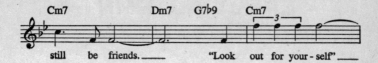

still be friends._____ "Look out for your-self"_____

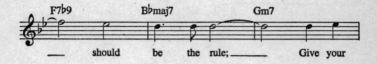

___ should be the rule;_____ Give your

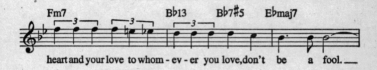

heart and your love to whom - ev - er you love, don't be a fool.____

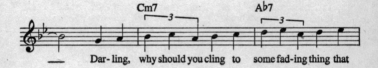

___ Dar-ling, why should you cling to some fad-ing thing that

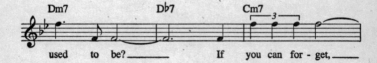

used to be?_____ If you can for - get,_____

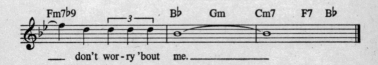

___ don't wor-ry 'bout me._____

EARLY AUTUMN

Words by JOHNNY MERCER
Music by RALPH BURNS and WOODY HERMAN

EASY TO LOVE
(You'd Be So Easy to Love)
from BORN TO DANCE

Words and Music by
COLE PORTER

Easy Swing

You'd be so eas - y to

love, so eas - y to

i - dol - ize, all oth - ers a - bove.

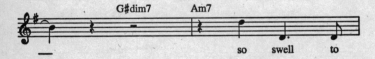

So worth the yearn - ing for, ____

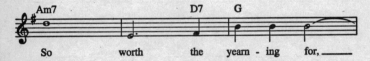

____ so swell to

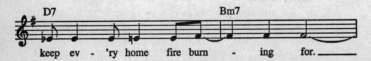

keep ev - 'ry home fire burn - ing for. ____

EVERYTHING HAPPENS TO ME

Words by TOM ADAIR
Music by MATT DENNIS

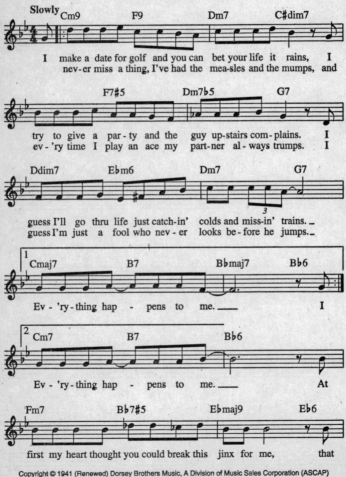

53

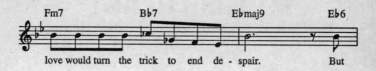

love would turn the trick to end de - spair.   But

now I just can't fool this head that thinks for me.   I've

mort-gaged all my cas - tles in the air.   I've

tel- e-graphed and phoned, I sent an "Air-mail Spe-cial" too,   your

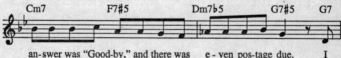

an-swer was "Good-by," and there was   e - ven pos-tage due.   I

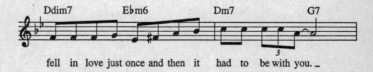

fell in love just once and then it   had to be with you. _

Ev - 'ry-thing hap - pens to   me. ____

FOOLISH HEART

from the Musical Production ONE TOUCH OF VENUS

Words by OGDEN NASH
Music by KURT WEILL

Slow Waltz tempo

Love should - n't be ser - ious, or

should it? You meet, per-haps you

kiss, you start._____ I fan - cied that

I un - der - stood it;_____ I for -

got my fool - ish heart._____ Love

can't be il - log - i - cal, can it?

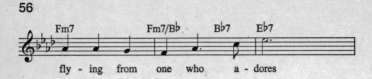

fly - ing from one who a - dores

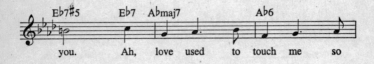

you. Ah, love used to touch me so

light - ly. Why will my heart be -

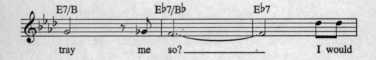

tray me so?_____ I would

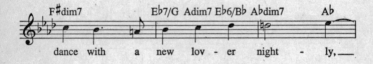

dance with a new lov - er night - ly,____

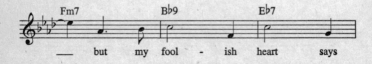

____ but my fool - ish heart says

no._____ Love no._____

GYPSY IN MY SOUL

Words by MOE JAFFE and CLAY BOLAND
Music by CLAY BOLAND

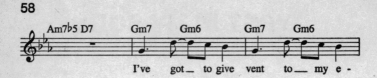
I've got_ to give vent to_ my e -

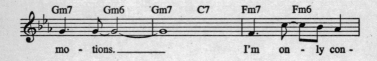
mo - tions._____ I'm on - ly con -

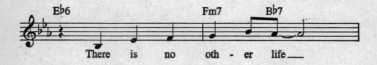
tent hav - ing my way._____

There is no oth - er life_

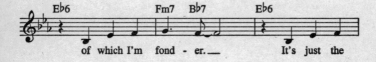
of which I'm fond - er._ It's just the

gyp - sy in_ my soul._____ No_ cares!_

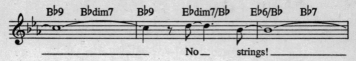

No— strings!—

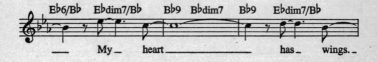

—My— heart— has— wings.—

— If I am

fan - cy free,— and love to wan - der,—

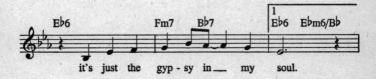

it's just the gyp - sy in— my soul.

soul.—

FOR ALL WE KNOW

Words by SAM M. LEWIS
Music by J. FRED COOTS

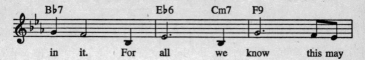

in it. For all we know this may

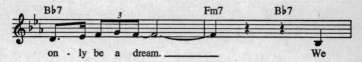

on - ly be a dream. _____ We

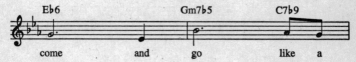

come and go like a

rip - ple on a stream. _____ So

love me to - night; to -

mor - row was made for some. To -

mor-row may nev - er come, for all we know.

For know. _____

THE FRIM FRAM SAUCE

Words and Music by JOE RICARDEL
and REDD EVANS

Moderate bounce

I don't want French fried po - ta - toes, red ripe to - ma - toes,
I'm nev - er sat - is - fied. ___ I want the
frim fram sauce with the aus - sen fay, ___ with cha -
fa - fa on the side. ___ I don't want
pork chops and ba - con; that won't a - wak - en
my ap - pe - tite ___ in - side. ___ I want the
frim fram sauce with the aus - sen fay, ___ with cha -

HAUNTED HEART

from INSIDE U.S.A.

Words by HOWARD DIETZ
Music by ARTHUR SCHWARTZ

Slowly and with expression

In the night ___ though we're a-part ___

there's a ghost of you with-in my haunt – ed heart. ___

___ Ghost of you ___ my lost ro – mance ___

___ lips that laugh, ___ eyes that dance,

___ haunt – ed heart ___ won't let me be. ___

65

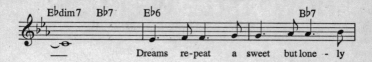

Dreams re-peat a sweet but lone-ly

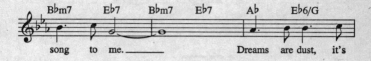

song to me. Dreams are dust, it's

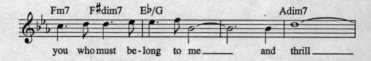

you who must be-long to me and thrill

my haunt-ed heart. Be still,

my haunt-ed heart.

heart.

HOW LITTLE WE KNOW

Words and Music by HOAGY CARMICHAEL
and JOHNNY MERCER

May-be it hap - pens this way, — may-be we real - ly be-long — to-geth-er, but af - ter all, ————— how lit-tle we know. ————— May-be it's just — for a day, — love is a change - a - ble as ——— the weath-er and af - ter all, ————— how lit-tle we know. —————

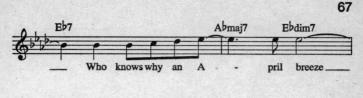

Who knows why an A - pril breeze _____

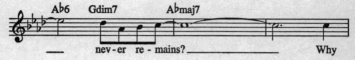

nev - er re - mains? _____ Why

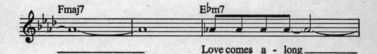

stars in the trees _____ hide when it rains? _

Love comes a - long _____

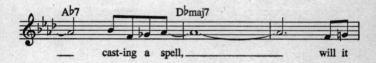

cast-ing a spell, _____ will it

sing you a song, _____ will it say a fare - well? _

Who can tell! May-be you're meant _ to be mine; _

68

I DON'T KNOW WHY
(I Just Do)

Lyric by ROY TURK
Music by FRED E. AHLERT

I CAN'T BELIEVE THAT YOU'RE IN LOVE WITH ME

**Words and Music by JIMMY McHUGH
and CLARENCE GASKILL**

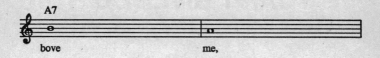

above me,

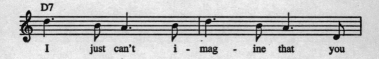

I just can't i - mag - ine that you

love me; And

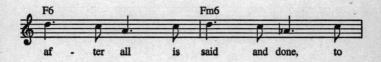

af - ter all is said and done, to

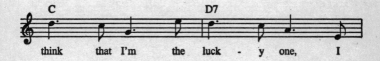

think that I'm the luck - y one, I

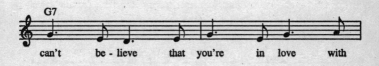

can't be - lieve that you're in love with

me.

I CAN'T GIVE YOU ANYTHING BUT LOVE

from BLACKBIRDS OF 1928

By JIMMY McHUGH
and DOROTHY FIELDS

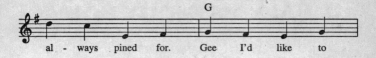

al - ways pined for. Gee I'd like to

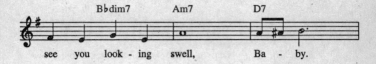

see you look - ing swell, Ba - by.

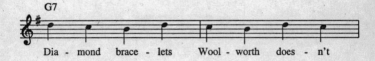

Dia - mond brace - lets Wool - worth does - n't

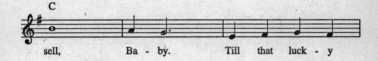

sell, Ba - by. Till that luck - y

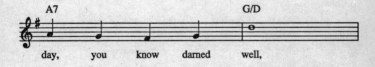

day, you know darned well,

Ba - by, I can't give you

an - y - thing but love. _____

I DON'T WANT TO
WALK WITHOUT YOU

from the Paramount Picture SWEATER GIRL

Words by FRANK LOESSER
Music by JULE STYNE

Slowly

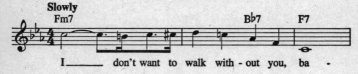

I___ don't want to walk with-out you, ba -

by, walk___ with-out my arm a - bout you,

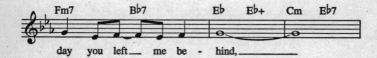

ba - by. I thought the

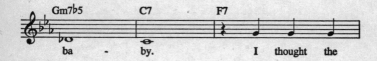

day you left___ me be - hind,___

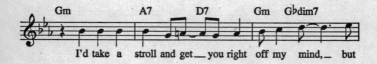

I'd take a stroll and get___ you right off my mind,___ but

now I find___ that I___ don't want to

walk with - out the sun - shine.

Why'd___ you have to turn off all that

sun - shine? Oh, ba - by

please come back___ or you'll break my heart for

me, 'Cause I___ don't want to

walk with - out you, no sir - ee.

I GET ALONG WITHOUT YOU VERY WELL
(Except Sometimes)

Words and Music by HOAGY CARMICHAEL
Inspired by a poem written by J.B. THOMPSON

I GUESS I'LL HANG MY TEARS OUT TO DRY

from GLAD TO SEE YOU

Words by SAMMY CAHN
Music by JULE STYNE

When I want rain, — I get sun-ny weath-er;
Friends ask me out, — I tell them I'm bus-y,

I'm just as blue as the sky. —
must get a new al-i-bi. —

Since love is gone, — can't pull my-self to-geth-er.
I stay at home, — and ask my-self where is {he? she?}

Guess I'll hang my tears out to dry. —

Guess I'll hang my tears out to dry. —

Dry lit-tle tear-drops, my lit-tle tear-drops,

I HADN'T ANYONE TILL YOU

Words and Music by
RAY NOBLE

I LOVE MY BABY
(My Baby Loves Me)
Words by BUD GREEN
Music by HARRY WARREN

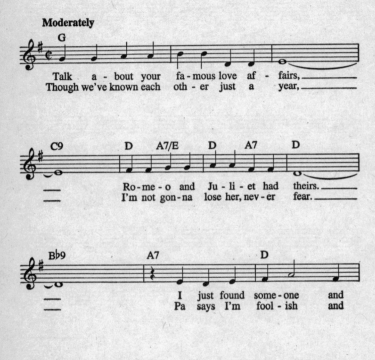

Talk a-bout your fa-mous love af-fairs,
Though we've known each oth-er just a year,

Ro-me-o and Ju-li-et had theirs.
I'm not gon-na lose her, nev-er fear.

I just found some-one and
Pa says I'm fool-ish and

some-one found me.
Ma says so, too,

We're not ver-y
'cause each eve-ning

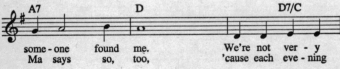

I WANNA BE LOVED

Words by BILLY ROSE and EDWARD HEYMAN
Music by JOHN GREEN

I wan - na be loved _____ with in - spi -
loved _____ with in - spi -

ra - tion, _____ I wan - na be loved start - ing to -
ra - tion, _____ I wan - na be loved start - ing to -

night. In - stead of mere - ly hold - ing con - ver -
night. In - stead of mere - ly hold - ing con - ver -

sa - tion _____ Hold me tight!
sa - tion _____ Hold me tight!

I wan - na be loved, _____ I crave af -
I wan - na be kissed _____ un - til I

F7   **C**

fec - tion,___ Those kiss - es of yours I'd glad - ly
tin - gle,___ I wan-na be kissed, start - ing to -

Ab7   **G7**   **Ab9**   **G7**   **C#dim7**

share,   I   want your eyes to shine in my di -
night,   Em - brace me till our heart - beats in - ter -

Dm7   **Dm7/G**   **C**   **Fm**

rec - tion.___ Make   me   care!_____
min - gle,___ Wrong   or   right._____

C   **C7**   **F**

___ I want the kind of ro - mance_ that should be
___ I'm in the mood to a - dore__ I'm read - y

         E7sus   **E7**

strong and e - qual - ly as ten - der._____
for that well - known tur - tle - dov - ing,_____

         Am   **E7**

___ I on - ly ask for the chance_ to know the
___ I'm in no mood to re - sist,___ and I in-

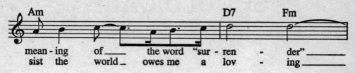

Am ... **D7** **Fm**

mean - ing   of____   the word "sur - ren - der"____
sist   the   world____ owes me   a   lov - ing____

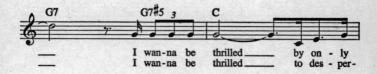

G7 ... **G7#5** 3 ... **C**

____   I wan-na be   thrilled____   by on - ly
____   I wan-na be   thrilled____   to des - per-

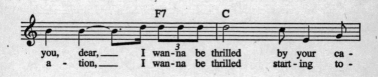

F7 ... **C**

you,   dear,____   I wan-na be thrilled   by your ca -
a - tion,____   I wan-na be thrilled   start-ing to-

Ab7 ... **G7** **Ab9** ... **G7** **C#dim7**

ress.   I   wan - na find   each dream of mine   come
night.   With   ev - 'ry kind   of won - der-ful   sen-

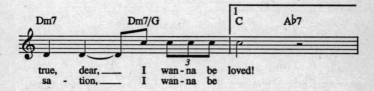

Dm7 ... **Dm7/G** | **1** **C** **Ab7**

true,   dear,____   I wan - na be loved!
sa - tion,____   I wan - na be

Dm7 **G7** **G7#5** 3 | **2** **C** **Fm** **C**

I wan-na be   loved!____

I SHOULD CARE

Words and Music by SAMMY CAHN,
PAUL WESTON and AXEL STORDAHL

I WISH I DIDN'T
LOVE YOU SO

from the Paramount Picture THE PERILS OF PAULINE

Words and Music by
FRANK LOESSER

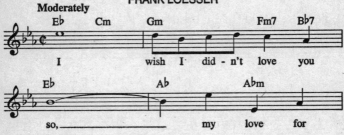

Moderately

I wish I did - n't love you

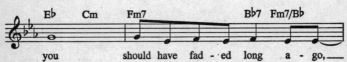

so, _____ my love for

you should have fad - ed long a - go, _____

you

I wish I did - n't need your

kiss. _____ Why must your

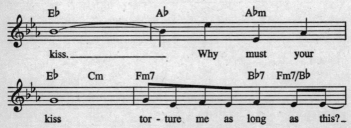

kiss tor - ture me as long as this? _____

I WON'T DANCE
from ROBERTA

Words and Music by JIMMY McHUGH, DOROTHY FIELDS,
JEROME KERN, OSCAR HAMMERSTEIN II and OTTO HARBACH

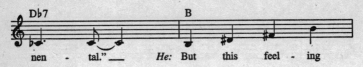

nen - tal." ___ *He:* But this feel - ing

is - n't pure - ly men - tal; ___

___ For heav - en rest us, ___

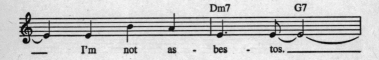

___ I'm not as - bes - tos. ___

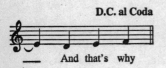

D.C. al Coda

___ And that's why

CODA

___ so if I

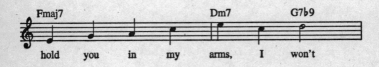

hold you in my arms, I won't

dance. ___

I'LL TAKE ROMANCE

Lyrics by OSCAR HAMMERSTEIN II
Music by BEN OAKLAND

Moderate Waltz

I'll take_____ ro -
I'll take_____ ro -

mance._____ While my
While my

heart is young and
arms are strong and

ea - ger to fly,
ea - ger for you,

I'll give my heart a
I'll give my arms their

try. I'll take ro -
cue. I'll take ro -

1 F | Dm7 | Gm7 | C11

mance._____

2 F | Gm7 | F

mance._____ So, my

lov - er, when you want me,

E♭m7 | A♭7

D♭maj7 | B♭m7 | E♭m7

call me in the

A♭11 | D♭maj7 | B♭m7

hush of the eve - ning.

G♭7 | C♭maj7

When you call

F | D7

me, in the hush of the

Gm7 | C9

eve - ning, I'll rush to my

first   real_____ ro -

mance._____ While   my

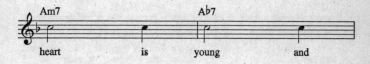

heart   is   young   and

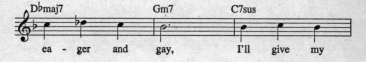

ea - ger   and   gay,   I'll   give   my

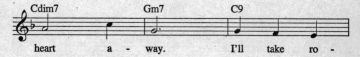

heart   a - way.   I'll   take   ro -

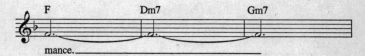

mance._____

I'll   take   my   own_____ ro -

mance._____

I'LL REMEMBER APRIL

Words and Music by PAT JOHNSON,
DON RAYE and GENE DE PAUL

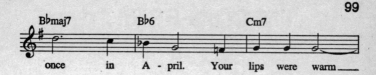

once in A - pril. Your lips were warm___

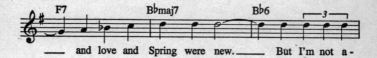

___ and love and Spring were new.___ But I'm not a-

fraid of Au - tumn and her sor - row,___

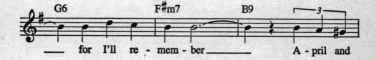

___ for I'll re - mem - ber___ A - pril and

you.___   won't for - get,___

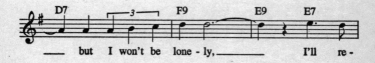

___ but I won't be lone - ly,___   I'll re-

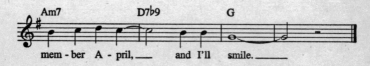

mem - ber A - pril,___ and I'll smile.___

I'M CONFESSIN'
(THAT I LOVE YOU)

Words and Music by AL NEIBURG,
DOC DOUGHERTY and ELLIS REYNOLDS

Slowly

I'm con-fess-in' that I love you.

Tell me, do you love me too?

I'm con-fess-in' that I need you, hon-est I

do, need you ev-'ry mo-ment.

In your eyes I read such strange things,

but your lips de-ny they're true.

Will your an-swer real-ly change things mak-ing me

I'M PUTTING ALL MY EGGS IN ONE BASKET

from the Motion Picture FOLLOW THE FLEET

Words and Music by
IRVING BERLIN

Moderately

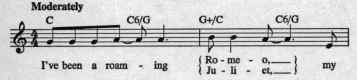

I've been a roam - ing { Ro - me - o,___ / Ju - li - et,___ } my

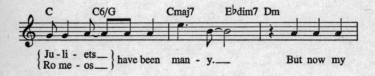

{ Ju - li - ets___ / Ro me - os___ } have been man - y.___ But now my

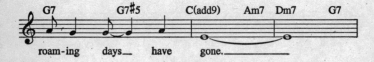

roam-ing days___ have gone.___

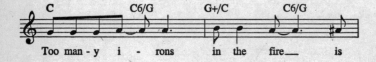

Too man-y i - rons in the fire___ is

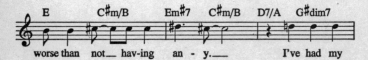

worse than not___ hav-ing an - y.___ I've had my

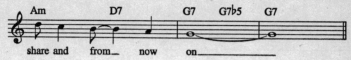

share and from now on

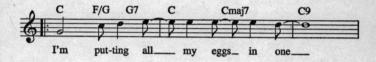

I'm put-ting all my eggs in one

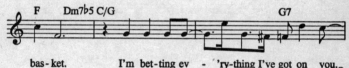

bas-ket. I'm bet-ting ev - 'ry-thing I've got on you.

I'm giv-ing all

my love to one ba - by.

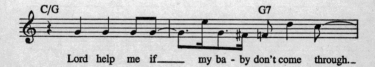

Lord help me if my ba - by don't come through.

IT'S A MOST UNUSUAL DAY

from A DATE WITH JUDY

Words by HAROLD ADAMSON
Music by JIMMY McHUGH

It's a most un - u - su - al
most un - u - su - al

day, _____ feel like throw - ing my
sky, _____ not a sign of a

wor - ries a - way, _____ as an
cloud pass - ing by, _____ and if

old na - tive born Cal - i - for - nian would
I want to sing, throw my heart in the

say, It's a most un - u - su - al

day. _____ There's a ring. It's a

106

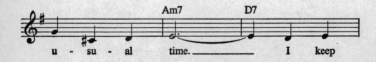

Am7 ... **D7** ... **G**
most un - u - su - al day._____

_____ **Em7** **E♭m7** **Dm7** ... **G7**
There are peo - ple_____ meet - ing

Cmaj7 ... **C6** **Em7** **E♭m7** **Dm7**
peo - ple,_____ there is sun - shine_____

G7 ... **Cmaj7** ... **C6** **F♯m7** **Fm7**
_____ ev - 'ry - where._____ There are

Em7 ... **A7** ... **Dmaj7**
peo - ple_____ greet - ing peo - ple_____

D6 ... **Am7/D** ... **D7**
_____ and a feel - ing of spring in the

Am7/D ... **D7** ... **F♯/G** **G**
air._____ It's a most un -

... **Am7** **D7**
u - su - al time._____ I keep

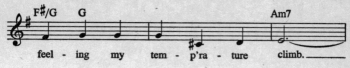

feel - ing my tem - p'ra - ture climb. ____

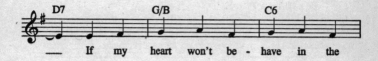

____ If my heart won't be - have in the

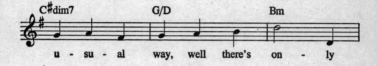

u - su - al way, well there's on - ly

one thing to say, ____ it's a

most un - u - su - al, most un -

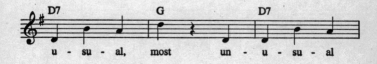

u - su - al, most un - u - su - al

day. ____

I'M SITTING ON TOP OF THE WORLD

from THE JOLSON STORY

Words by SAM M. LEWIS and JOE YOUNG
Music by RAY HENDERSON

Par, get read - y to call."

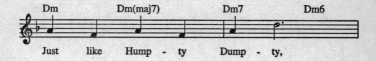

Just like Hump - ty Dump - ty,

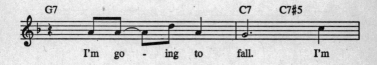

I'm go - ing to fall. I'm

sit - ting on top of the

world, _____ just roll - ing a -

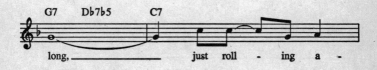

long, _____ just roll - ing a -

long. _____

IF I SHOULD LOSE YOU

from the Paramount Picture ROSE OF THE RANCHO

Words and Music by LEO ROBIN
and RALPH RAINGER

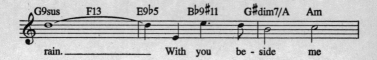

rain. _____ With you be - side me

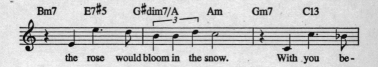

the rose would bloom in the snow. With you be-

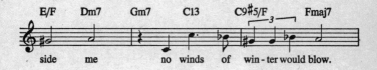

side me no winds of win - ter would blow.

I gave you my love _____ and I was

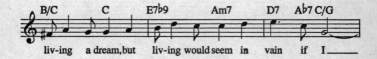

liv-ing a dream, but liv-ing would seem in vain if I _____

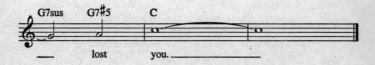

_____ lost you. _____

IMAGINATION

Words by JOHNNY BURKE
Music by JIMMY VAN HEUSEN

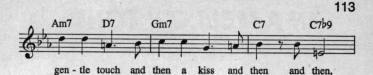

gen - tle touch and then a kiss and then and then,

find it's on - ly your i - mag - i - na - tion a - gain? Oh,

well, i - mag - i - na - tion is sil - ly, You

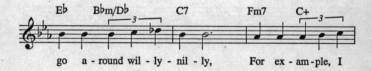

go a - round wil - ly - nil - ly, For ex - am - ple, I

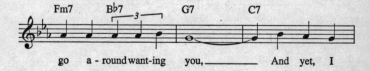

go a - round want - ing you, _____ And yet, I

can't i - mag - ine that you want me too. _____

IN A MELLOW TONE

Words by MILT GABLER
Music by DUKE ELLINGTON

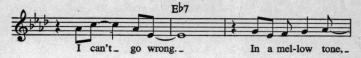

I can't go wrong. In a mel-low tone,

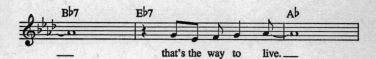

that's the way to live.

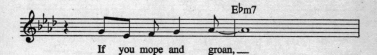

If you mope and groan,

some-thing's got to give.

So go your way and laugh and play.

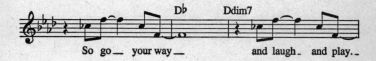

There's joy un-known

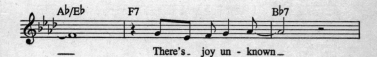

in a mel-low tone.

IN A SENTIMENTAL MOOD

Words and Music by DUKE ELLINGTON,
IRVING MILLS and MANNY KURTZ

Slowly

In a sen-ti-men-tal mood

I can see the stars come thru my room,

while your lov-ing at-ti-tude is like a

flame that lights the

gloom. On the wings of ev-'ry kiss

drifts a mel-o-dy so strange and sweet,

in this sen-ti-men-tal bliss you make my

IN LOVE IN VAIN

Words by LEO ROBIN
Music by JEROME KERN

Slowly, lyrically

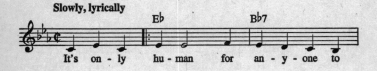

It's on-ly hu-man for an-y-one to

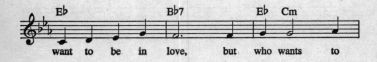

want to be in love, but who wants to

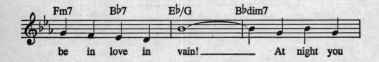

be in love in vain! _____ At night you

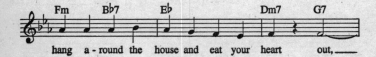

hang a-round the house and eat your heart out, ___

___ and cry your eyes out _____ and wrack your

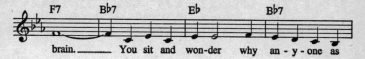

brain._____ You sit and won-der why an-y-one as

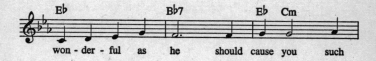

won-der-ful as he should cause you such

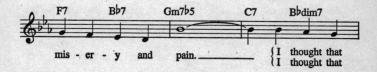

mis-er-y and pain._____ { I thought that \ I thought that }

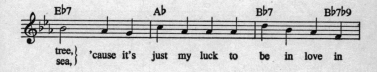

I would be in heav-en, but I'm on-ly up a
I'd have eas-y sail-ing but in-stead, I'm all at

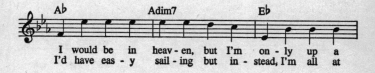

tree,} 'cause it's just my luck to be in love in
sea,}

vain. It's on-ly vain._____

IN THE BLUE OF EVENING

Words by TOM ADAIR
Music by D'ARTEGA

121

IT ONLY HAPPENS WHEN
I DANCE WITH YOU

from the Motion Picture Irving Berlin's EASTER PARADE

Words and Music by
IRVING BERLIN

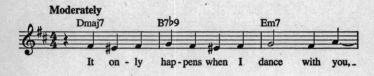

It on-ly hap-pens when I dance with you,—

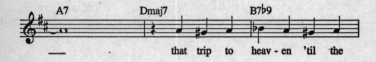

— that trip to heav-en 'til the

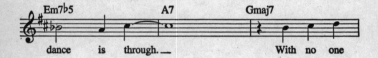

dance is through.— With no one

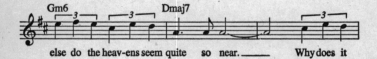

else do the heav-ens seem quite so near.—— Why does it

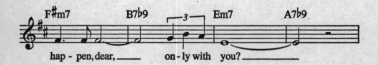

hap-pen, dear, —— on-ly with you?————

Dmaj7 B7♭9 Em7
Two cheeks to - geth - er can be so di - vine, –
A7 Dmaj7 B7♭9
— but on - ly when those cheeks are
Em7♭5 A7 Gmaj7
yours and mine. — I've danced with
Gm6 F#m7♭5 B7#5
3 3
doz - ens of oth - ers the whole night through,
Em7 A7 D F#m7
but the thrill that comes with spring when an - y - thing could
B7 Em7 A11 A7
hap - pen, that on - ly hap - pens with
1 D6 Bm9 Em7 A7
you. —
2 D6
you. —

IT'S A BLUE WORLD

Words and Music by BOB WRIGHT
and CHET FORREST

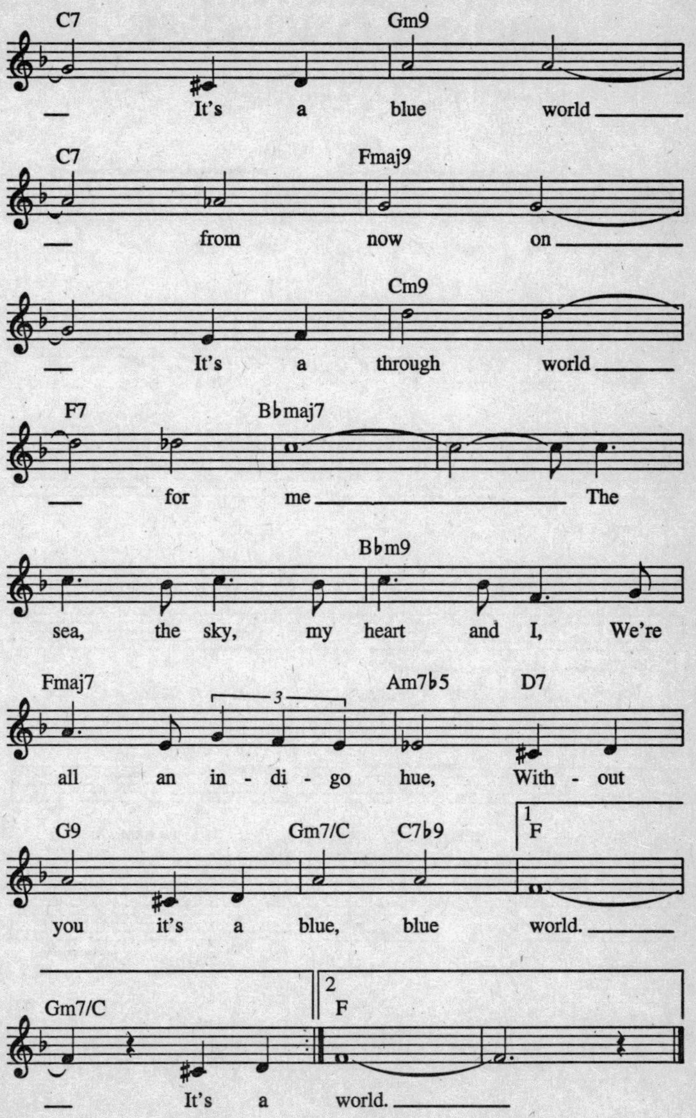

C7 Gm9
— It's a blue world ___
C7 Fmaj9
— from now on ___
Cm9
— It's a through world ___
F7 B♭maj7
— for me ___ The
B♭m9
sea, the sky, my heart and I, We're
Fmaj7 Am7♭5 D7
all an in - di - go hue, With - out
G9 Gm7/C C7♭9 1 F
you it's a blue, blue world. ___
Gm7/C 2 F
— It's a world. ___

IT'S BEEN A
LONG, LONG TIME

Lyric by SAMMY CAHN
Music by JULE STYNE

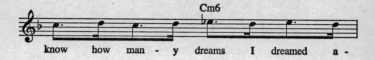

know how man - y dreams I dreamed a -

bout you _____ or

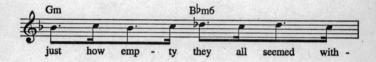

just how emp - ty they all seemed with -

out you. _____ So,

kiss me once, then kiss me twice, then

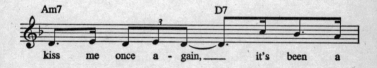

kiss me once a - gain, ____ it's been a

long, long time.

IVY

from the Motion Picture IVY

Words and Music by
HOAGY CARMICHAEL

129

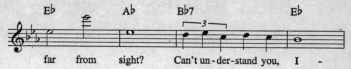
far from sight? Can't un-der-stand you, I-

vy. But re - mem - ber this: If you

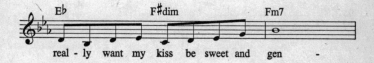
real - ly want my kiss be sweet and gen -

tle, lest we part.____ Re-mem - ber,____

__ re - mem - ber ____ (I - vy.)

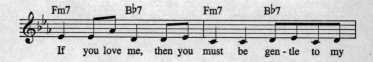
If you love me, then you must be gen - tle to my

heart, I - vy. ____

JUST SQUEEZE ME
(But Don't Tease Me)
Words by LEE GAINES
Music by DUKE ELLINGTON

sing - ing the blues a - way each day,

B♭

count - ing the nights and wait - ing for you. __

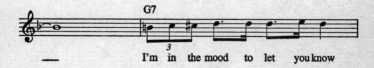

__ I'm in the mood to let you know

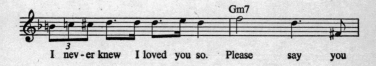

Gm7

I nev - er knew I loved you so. Please say you

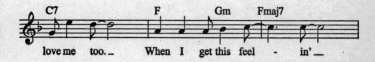

C7   F   Gm   Fmaj7

love me too. __ When I get this feel - in' __

F   Gm   Fmaj7   F#dim7   Am/G   Gm/C

I'm in ec - sta - sy. __ So __ squeeze __ me, __

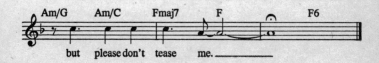

Am/G   Am/C   Fmaj7   F   F6

but please don't tease me. __

THE LAST TIME
I SAW PARIS

from LADY, BE GOOD
from TILL THE CLOUDS ROLL BY

Lyrics by OSCAR HAMMERSTEIN II
Music by JEROME KERN

Moderately

The last time I saw Par - is her

heart was warm and gay. I heard the laugh - ter

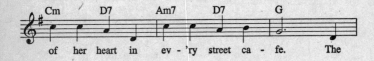

of her heart in ev - 'ry street ca - fe. The

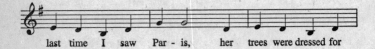

last time I saw Par - is, her trees were dressed for

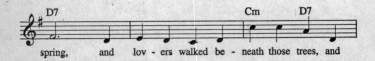

spring, and lov - ers walked be - neath those trees, and

LAZYBONES

**Words and Music by HOAGY CARMICHAEL
and JOHNNY MERCER**

La - zy bones, sleep - in' in the sun,
La - zy bones, sleep - in' in the shade,

how you 'spec' to get your day's work done?
how you 'spec' to get your corn - meal made?

Nev - er get your day's work done,
Nev - er get your corn - meal made

sleep - in' in the noon - day sun.
sleep - in' in the eve - nin'

shade. _____ When 'tat - ers need spray - in', I

135

LEARNIN' THE BLUES

Words and Music by
DOLORES "VICKI" SILVERS

in a crowd, the blues will taunt you con-stant-ly.

When you're out in a crowd, the blues will haunt your mem-o-

ry. The nights when you don't sleep, ____

____ the whole night you're cry-in'. But you can't for-

get { her, ____ / him, ____ } soon you e-ven stop try-in'.

You'll walk the floor ____ and wear out your

shoes. When you feel your heart break, ____

____ you're learn-in' the blues. ____

LET THERE BE LOVE

Lyric by IAN GRANT
Music by LIONEL RAND

LET'S FACE THE MUSIC AND DANCE

from the Motion Picture FOLLOW THE FLEET

Words and Music by
IRVING BERLIN

Moderately

Cm   **Ab/C**   **Cm**
There may be trou - ble a -

Cm6   **Cm7**   **Cm**
head. _____ But while there's

Ab/C   **Cm**   **Dm7b5**   **G7**
moon - light and mu - sic and

C   **Cmaj7**   **C7**
love and ro - mance, _____

F6   **Fm6**
let's face the mu - sic and dance. __

C   **Ab9**   **Dm7b5**   **G7#5**   **Cm**
Be - fore the

Ab/C   **Cm**   **Cm6**   **Cm7**
fid - dlers have fled, _____

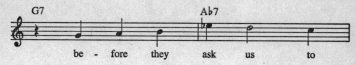

be - fore they ask us to

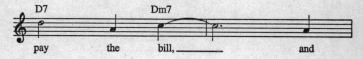

pay the bill,_____ and

while we still ____ have the chance, __

____ let's face the

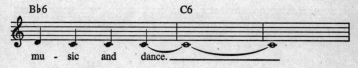

mu - sic and dance._____

Soon _____ we'll be with -

out the moon, ____ hum - ming a

dif - f'rent tune, ____ and

142

LOVER
from the Paramount Picture LOVE ME TONIGHT

Lyrics by LORENZ HART
Music by RICHARD RODGERS

Gm7　　　　　C7　　　　　F#m7

glanc - ing _____ in my eyes _____
quar - rel _____ with our bliss _____

B7　　　　Fm7　　　　Bb7

_____ till love's _____ own en-
_____ when two _____ lips of

Em7　　　　　A7　　　　D

tranc - ing _____ mu - sic dies. _____
cor - al _____ want to kiss? _____

_____
_____

F#　　　　　　　G#m7

All of my fu - ture is in you. _____
I say, "The Dev - il is in you", _____

C#7　　　F#

_____ Your ev - 'ry plan I de -
_____ and to re - sist you I

G#m7　　　C#7　　　　A

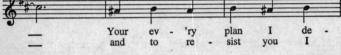

sign. _____ Prom - ise you'll
try; _____ but if you

Bm7　　　　E7

al - ways con - tin - ue _____ to be
did - n't con - tin - ue _____ I would

mine. _____
die! _____

Lov - er, _____ please be

ten - der._____ When you're ten - der, _____

_____ fears de - part. _____

Lov - er, _____ I sur -

ren - der _____ to my heart._____

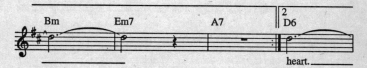

heart._____

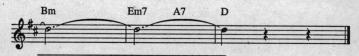

LET'S FALL IN LOVE

Words by TED KOEHLER
Music by HARLOLD ARLEN

Moderately bright

Let's fall in love. Why should-n't we_ _ fall in love? Our hearts are made_ _ of it. Let's take a chance._ Why be a-fraid_ _ of it?_

Let's close our eyes, and make our own_ _ par - a - dise. Lit - tle we know_ _ of it, still we can try_ to make a go_

LET'S GET AWAY FROM IT ALL

Words and Music by TOM ADAIR
and MATT DENNIS

vis - it   ev - 'ry   state.   A -

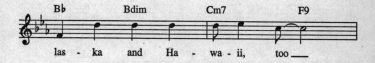

las - ka   and   Ha - wa - ii,   too___

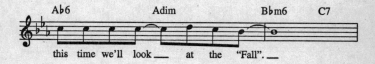

then   all   the   fort - y - eight.___

Let's   go   a - gain___   to   Ni - a -   g'ra, ___

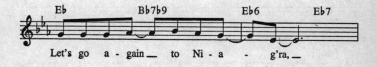

this   time   we'll   look ___   at   the   "Fall". ___

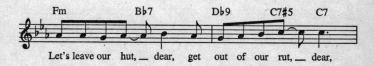

Let's   leave   our   hut, ___   dear,   get   out   of   our   rut, ___   dear,

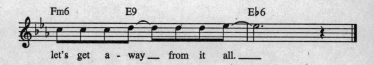

let's   get   a - way___   from   it   all. ___

150 LIKE SOMEONE IN LOVE

Words by JOHNNY BURKE
Music by JIMMY VAN HEUSEN

Late - ly I find my - self out
gaz - ing at stars,
hear - ing gui - tars like
some - one in love.
Some - times the things I do a -
stound me, _____
most - ly when - ev - er you're a -
round me. Late - ly I

seem to walk as though I had wings, bump in - to things like some - one in love. Each time I look at you I'm limp as a glove and feel - ing like some - one in love. love. love._____

LITTLE WHITE LIES

Words and Music by
WALTER DONALDSON

Easy Swing

Amaj7   Dm7   G7   Amaj7

The moon was all a - glow,   and heav-en was in your

Dm7   G7   C#m7   F#7   Bm7   E7

eyes,   the night _ that you told me

Bm7   E7   Amaj7   Bm7 E7   Amaj7

those lit - tle white lies. ___ The stars all seemed to

Dm7   G7   Amaj7   Dm7   G7

know   that you did-n't mean all those sighs,

C#m7   F#7   Bm7   E7   Bm7   E7

the night _ that you told me those lit - tle white

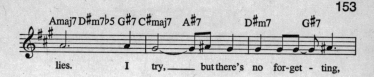

lies. I try, ___ but there's no for-get - ting,

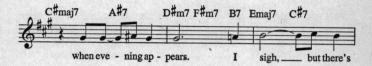

when eve - ning ap - pears. I sigh, ___ but there's

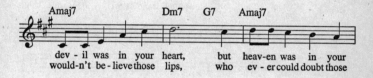

no re-gret - ting, in spite _ of my tears. { The
{ Who

dev - il was in your heart, but heav-en was in your
would-n't be - lieve those lips, who ev - er could doubt those

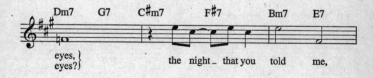

eyes, }
eyes? } the night _ that you told me,

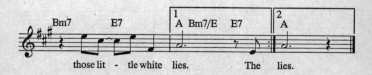

those lit - tle white lies. The lies.

LOVE IS THE SWEETEST THING

Words and Music by
RAY NOBLE

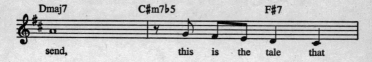

Dmaj7   **C#m7b5**   **F#7**

send,   this   is   the   tale   that

Bm7   **E7**

nev - er   will   tire,   this   is   the   song   with - out

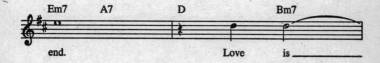

Em7   **A7**   **D**   **Bm7**

end.   Love   is _____

Em7   **A7**

___   the   great   -   est   thing,

D   **Bm7**   **Em7**   **A7**

the   old - est,   yet   the   lat - est thing,

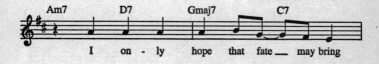

Am7   **D7**   **Gmaj7**   **C7**

I   on - ly   hope   that   fate ___ may bring

Bm7   **E7**   **A7**   **D**

love's   sto - ry   to   you.

MAKIN' WHOOPEE!

from WHOOPEE!

Lyrics by GUS KAHN
Music by WALTER DONALDSON

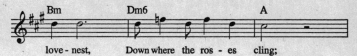

love - nest,   Down where the ros - es   cling;

Pic-ture the same sweet love-nest,   think what a year can

bring._____ He's wash-ing dish - es_____ and ba - by

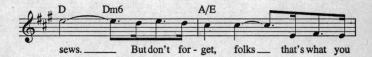

clothes _____ he's so am - bi - tious___ he e - ven

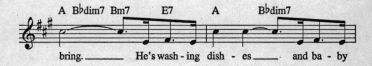

sews. _____   But don't for - get, folks __ that's what you

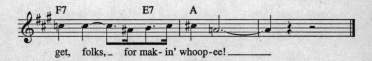

get, folks, _ for mak- in' whoop-ee! _____

MIDNIGHT SUN

Words and Music by LIONEL HAMPTON,
SONNY BURKE and JOHNNY MERCER

Slowly, with a beat

Your lips were like a red and ru - by chal - ice, warm - er than the sum - mer night, _____ the clouds were like an al - a - bas - ter pal - ace ris - ing to a snow - y height. _____ Each star its own au - ro - ra bo - re - al - is; sud - den - ly you held me tight. _____ I could see the

Dmaj7　　　D6　　　G#m7　　　C#7b9

mid - night　　sun. ____

F#maj7　　　F#6　　　F#m7　　　B7

Was there such a night? It's a thrill I still don't quite be -

Emaj7　　　E6　　　Emaj7　　　E6

lieve, _____　　but

Emaj7　　　E6　　　Emaj7　　　A9 A7#5

af - ter you were gone, there was still some star - dust on my sleeve. _

F#m7　　　F9　　　Em7　　　Eb7#9

_____　　The

D

flame of it may dwin - dle to an em - ber,　and the stars for-

Dm7　　　G9　　　Dm7　　　G9

get to shine, _____　　and

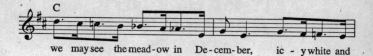

we may see the mead-ow in De-cem-ber, ic-y white and

crys - tal - line. _____ But,

oh, my dar-ling, al-ways I'll re-mem-ber when your lips were

close to mine _____ and { I we } saw the

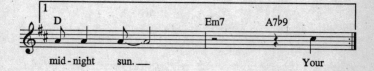

mid-night sun. __

mid-night sun. _____

MY BABY JUST CARES FOR ME

from WHOOPEE!

Lyrics by GUS KAHN
Music by WALTER DONALDSON

my ba-by don't care for high - toned

D.C. al Coda

plac - es.

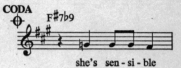

CODA

F#7b9

she's sen - si - ble

F#7 Bm7 G#7

as can be. My ba-by don't

C#m7 F#7 Bm7

care who knows it, My ba-by just

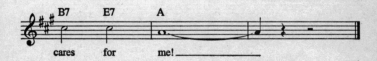

B7 E7 A

cares for me!

MY SHIP
from the Musical Production LADY IN THE DARK
Words by IRA GERSHWIN
Music by KURT WEILL

Moderately slow

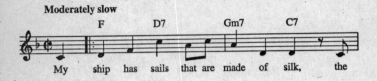

My ship has sails that are made of silk, the

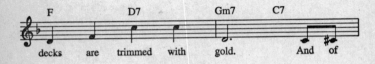

decks are trimmed with gold. And of

jam and spice there's a par - a - dise in the

hold. _____ My ship's a - glow with a

mil - lion pearls and ru - bies fill each

165

bin; the sun sits high in a

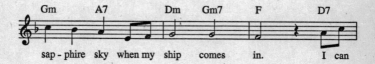

sap - phire sky when my ship comes in. I can

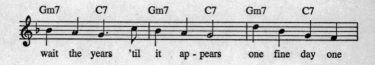

wait the years 'til it ap - pears one fine day one

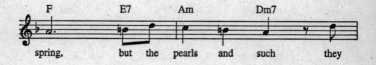

spring, but the pearls and such they

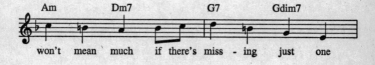

won't mean much if there's miss - ing just one

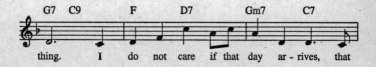

thing. I do not care if that day ar - rives, that

166

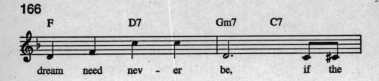

| F | D7 | Gm7 | C7 |

dream   need   nev - er   be,   if the

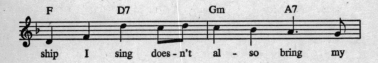

| F | D7 | Gm | A7 |

ship   I   sing   does-n't   al - so   bring   my

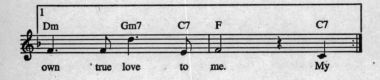

1

| Dm | Gm7 | C7 | F | C7 |

own   'true   love   to   me.   My

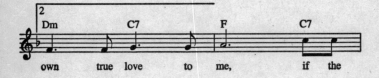

2

| Dm | C7 | F | C7 |

own   true   love   to   me,   if the

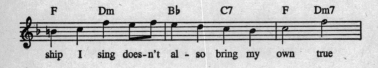

| F | Dm | Bb | C7 | F | Dm7 |

ship   I   sing does-n't   al - so   bring   my   own   true

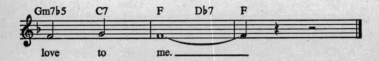

| Gm7b5 | C7 | F | Db7 | F |

love   to   me. _____

MY BUDDY

Lyrics by GUS KAHN
Music by WALTER DONALDSON

Slowly

Nights are long since you went a -
Miss are your voice, since the touch of your

way, I think a - bout you
hand, Just long to know you that

all thru the day; } My
you un - der - stand; }

Bud - dy, _____ My

Bud - dy, _____ { No
Your } Bud - dy

1
quite so true. _____

2
miss - es you. _____

MY IDEAL
from the Paramount Picture PLAYBOY OF PARIS

Words by LEO ROBIN
Music by RICHARD A. WHITING and NEWELL CHASE

Slowly

Will I ev - er find the

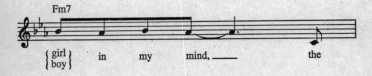

{ girl / boy } in my mind, _____ the

one who is my ___ i - deal?

May - be { she's / he's } a dream and

yet { she / he } might be ___ just a - round the cor - ner

F#m7   B7   Fm7   Bb7

wait - ing   for   me. ___

Ebmaj7   C7

Will   I   rec - og - nize   a

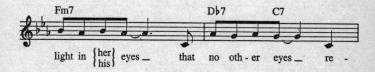

Fm7   Db7   C7

light in {her/his} eyes __   that   no oth - er   eyes __   re -

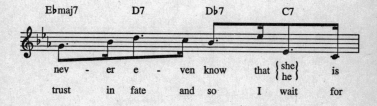

F7   Fm7   Abm7   Db7

veal,   {or / al - tho'}   {will I pass {her/him} by and / {she/he} may be late,   I}

Ebmaj7   D7   Db7   C7

nev - er   e - ven   know   that {she/he}   is
trust   in   fate   and   so   I   wait   for

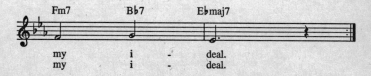

Fm7   Bb7   Ebmaj7

my   i - deal.
my   i - deal.

MY OLD FLAME

from the Paramount Picture BELLE OF THE NINETIES
Words and Music by ARTHUR JOHNSTON
and SAM COSLOW

Moderately

My old flame, __ I can't e-ven think __ of his name __ but it's fun-ny now and then, how my thoughts go flash-ing back a-gain, __ to my old flame. __ My old flame, __ my new lov-ers all __ seem so tame. __ For I have-n't met a gent so mag-nif-i-cent or el-e-gant __ as

my old flame.___ I've met so man-y who had

fas-ci-nat-in' ways,_ a fas-cin-at-in' gaze_ in their eyes;_

_____ some who took me up___ to the skies._

_____ But their at-tempts at love were

on-ly im-i-ta-tions of my old flame,___ I

can't e-ven think_ of his name._____ But I'll

nev-er be the same un-til I dis-cov-er what be-came_ of

my old flame. flame.

NANCY - WITH THE LAUGHING FACE

Words by PHIL SILVERS
Music by JAMES VAN HEUSEN

Cm(maj7)   Cm7

- ing?   Well, she'll give you the ver - y same glow.
— to,   when the long day has drawn to a close.

F9   F7b5 Abm   Eb/Bb

— When she speaks you would think_ it was sing -
— There's the pat - ter of feet_ to come home

Fm7   Bb7   G7#5   Cm   Cm7   F7

- ing,   just   hear   her   say,   "Hel -
— to,   and   Nan - cy   gave   me

Bb7sus Bb7 Edim   Fm7

lo."   I swear to   good-ness you can't_   re -
those.   Keep Bet - ty   Gra - ble, La - mour_   and

Bb9   Eb

sist   her,   sor - ry for   you_   she
Turn - er,   she makes my   heart_   a

D   F#m   Fm

has   no   sis - ter.)
char - coal   burn - er.)   No one could ev - er re - place_

Dm7b5   G7#5   G7   Cm   Abm

— my   Nan - cy with the laugh-ing   face.

1. Eb   G7#5   2. Eb   Ab6   Eb6

— What a   —

THE NEARNESS OF YOU

from the Paramount Picture ROMANCE IN THE DARK

Words by NED WASHINGTON
Music by HOAGY CARMICHAEL

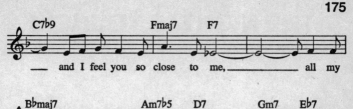

and I feel you so close to me,_____ all my

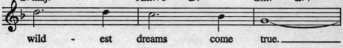

wild - est dreams come true._____

I need no soft lights to en - chant me if

you'll on - ly grant me the right_____

to hold you ev - er so tight,_____ and to feel in the

night the near - ness of you._____

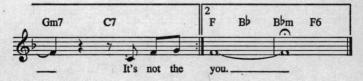

It's not the you._____

THE NIGHT IS YOUNG
(And You're So Beautiful)

Words by BILLY ROSE and IRVING KAHAL
Music by DANA SUESSE

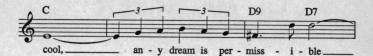

cool,_____ an - y dream is per - miss - i - ble_____

___ in the heart of a fool._____ The

moon is high and you're so glam-or- ous, and if I seem

o - ver-am-or- ous, la - dy,_____ what can I

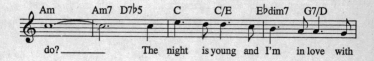

do?_____ The night is young and I'm in love with

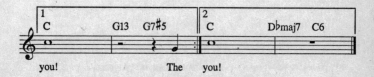

you! The you!

OL' MAN RIVER

from SHOW BOAT
Lyrics by OSCAR HAMMERSTEIN II
Music by JEROME KERN

Very slowly

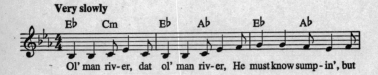

Ol' man riv-er, dat ol' man riv-er, He must know sump-in', but

don't say noth-in', He jus' keeps roll-in', He keeps on roll-in' a-

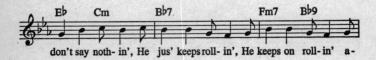

long. _____ He don't plant 'ta-ters, he

don't plant cot-ton, An' dem dat plants 'em is soon for-got-ten; But

ol' man riv-er, he jus' keeps roll-in' a-long. _____

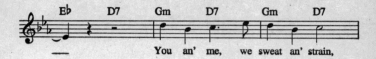

You an' me, we sweat an' strain,

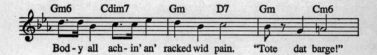

Bod-y all ach-in' an' racked wid pain. "Tote dat barge!"

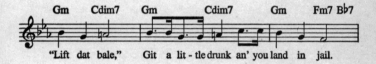

"Lift dat bale," Git a lit-tle drunk an' you land in jail.

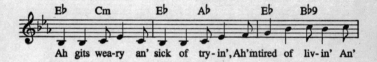

Ah gits wea-ry an' sick of try-in', Ah'm tired of liv-in' An'

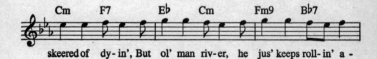

skeered of dy-in', But ol' man riv-er, he jus' keeps roll-in' a-

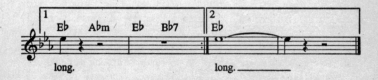

long.   long. _____

ON THE SUNNY SIDE
OF THE STREET

Lyric by DOROTHY FIELDS
Music by JIMMY McHUGH

Moderately

C / E7

Grab your coat, and get your hat Leave your

F / G7 / Am

wor - ry on the door - step Just di - rect your

D7 / Dm7 / G7

feet To the sun - ny side __ of the

C / G7 / C

street. Can't you hear a pit - ter -

E7 / F

pat? And that hap - py tune is

G7 / Am / D7

your step. Life can be so sweet On the

Dm7 / G7 / C

sun - ny side __ of the street. I used to

ONCE IN LOVE WITH AMY
from WHERE'S CHARLEY?

By FRANK LOESSER

Slow and easy Soft-Shoe

Once in love with A-my, ___
Once you're kissed by A-my, ___

Al - ways in love with A - my. ___
tear up your list, it's A - my. ___

Ev - er and ev - er fas - ci - nat - ed by 'er,
Ply her with bon-bons, po - et - ry and flow - ers,

sets your heart a - fire ___ to stay.
moon a mil - lion hours ___ a -

way. You might be quite the fick - le-heart - ed

rov - er, so care - free and bold who

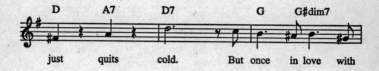

loves a girl and la - ter thinks it o - ver and

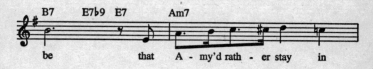

just quits cold. But once in love with

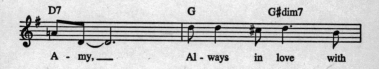

A - my, ____ Al - ways in love with

A - my. ____ Ev - er and ev - er

sweet - ly you'll ro-mance 'er. Trou - ble is, the an - swer will

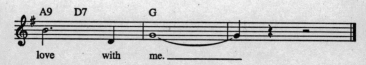

be that A - my'd rath - er stay in

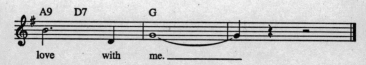

love with me. _____

ONE MORNING IN MAY

Words by MITCHELL PARISH
Music by HOAGY CARMICHAEL

Moderately

One   morn - ing   in   May,   don't for -
One   morn - ing   in   May,   oh   the
One   morn - ing   in   May   to   re -

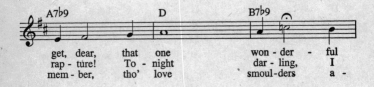

get, dear,   that   one   won - der - ful
rap - ture!   To - night   dar - ling,   I
mem - ber,   tho'   love   smoul-ders   a -

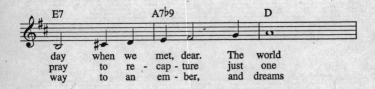

day   when   we   met, dear.   The   world
pray   to   re - cap - ture   just   one
way   to   an   em - ber,   and   dreams

To Coda ⊕

o - ver   was   blue   clo - ver,   and
hour,   just   one   flow - er   from
per - ish,   we'll   still   cher - ish   that

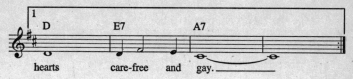

1
D · · · E7 · · · A7
hearts · · · care-free · and · gay._____

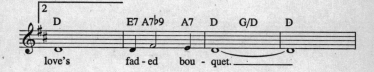

2
D · · · E7 · A7♭9 · A7 · D · G/D · D
love's · · · fad-ed · bou-quet._____

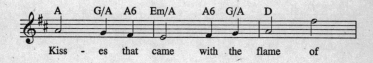

A · G/A · A6 · Em/A · A6 · G/A · D
Kiss - es · that · came · with · the · flame · of

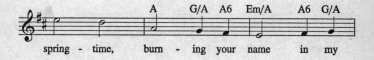

A · G/A · A6 · Em/A · A6 · G/A
spring - time, · burn - ing · your · name · in · my

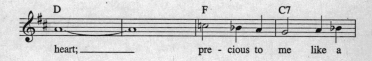

D · · · F · · · C7
heart;_____ · pre - cious · to · me · like · a

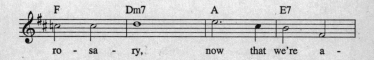

F · · · Dm7 · · · A · · · E7
ro - sa - ry, · · · now · that · we're · a -

186

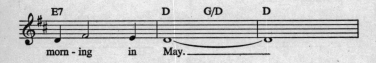

part. ____

CODA

one

morn - ing   in   May. ____

Pale   cheeks   so   soft,   *(and   white)*

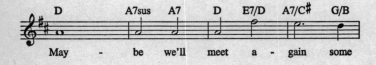

where   do   you   dream? *(to - night?)* ___

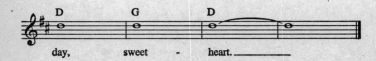

May -   be   we'll   meet   a - gain   some

day,   sweet -   heart. ____

ROBBIN'S NEST

By SIR CHARLES THOMPSON
and "ILLINOIS" JACQUET

PUT YOUR DREAMS AWAY
(For Another Day)
featured in THE FRANK SINATRA SHOW

Lyric by RUTH LOWE
Music by STEPHAN WEISS and PAUL MANN

When your dreams at night fade be -

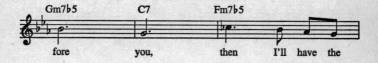

fore you, then I'll have the

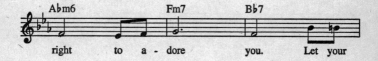

right to a - dore you. Let your

kiss con - fess, this is

hap - pi - ness, dar - ling, and

put all your dreams a - way.

Put your way.

ROCKIN' CHAIR

Words and Music by
HOAGY CARMICHAEL

Moderately

Old rock-in' chair's got me, _____ cane by my side. Fetch me that gin, son, 'fore I tan your hide. Can't get from this cab-in, _____ goin' no - where. Just sit me here grab-bin' at the flies 'round this rock-in'

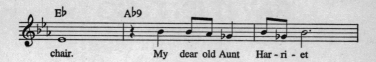

chair.　　My　dear old Aunt　Har‑ri‑et

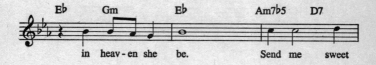

in　heav‑en she　be.　　Send me　　sweet

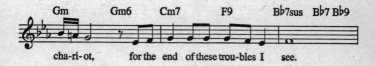

cha‑ri‑ot,　　for the end of these trou‑bles I　see.

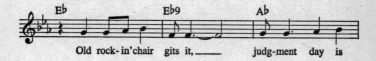

Old rock‑in'chair gits it,＿＿＿　judg‑ment day is

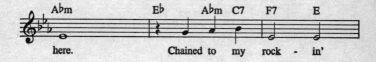

here.　　Chained to　my　rock‑in'

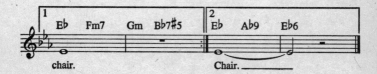

chair.　　Chair.＿＿＿

SAY IT ISN'T SO

Words and Music by
IRVING BERLIN

Moderately

Say it is-n't so, _____ Say it is-n't so. _____

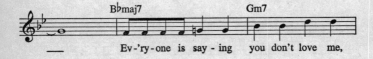

_____ Ev-'ry-one is say-ing you don't love me,

Say it is-n't so. _____ Ev-'ry-where I go, _____

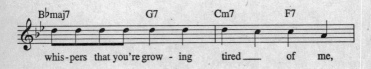

_____ ev-'ry-one I know _____

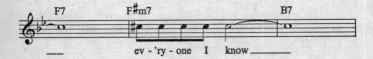

whis-pers that you're grow - ing tired _____ of me,

193

Say it is-n't so.____ Peo-ple say that you____

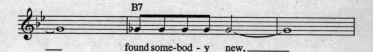

____ found some-bod - y new,_____

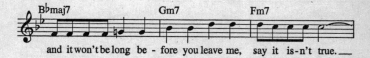

and it won't be long be - fore you leave me, say it is-n't true. ____

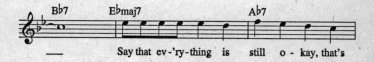

____ Say that ev-'ry-thing is still o - kay, that's

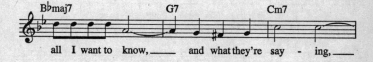

all I want to know,____ and what they're say - ing,____

____ Say it is - n't so._____

SAY IT WITH MUSIC

from the 1921 Stage Production MUSIC BOX REVUE
from the 20th Century Fox Motion Picture
ALEXANDER'S RAGTIME BAND

Words and Music by
IRVING BERLIN

Mu - sic is a lang - uage lov - ers un - der-
There's a ten - der mes - sage deep down in my

stand. Mel - o - dy and ro - mance
heart. Some - thing you should know, but

wan - der hand in hand. Cu - pid nev - er
how am I to start? Sen - ti - men - tal

fails as - sis - ted by a band.
speech - es nev - er could im - part

So if you have some - thing sweet to
just ex - act - ly what I want to

tell her: } Say it with mu -
tell you: }

sic, beau - ti - ful mu -

195

SENTIMENTAL ME

Words by JIMMY CASSIN
Music by JIM MOREHEAD

Moderately

Sen - ti - men - tal me

guess I'll al - ways be

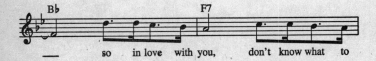

so in love with you, don't know what to

do, sen - ti - men - tal me

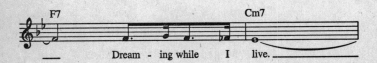

Dream - ing while I live.

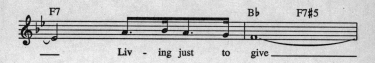

F7   Bb   F7#5

— Liv - ing just to give _____

Bb   F7

— all my love to you, no one else will

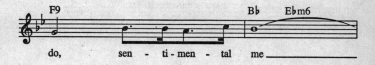

F9   Bb   Ebm6

do, sen - ti - men - tal me _____

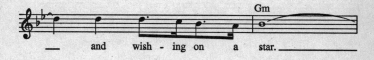

Bb   D7

— Reach - ing for the moon _____

Gm

— and wish - ing on a star. _____

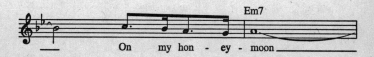

Em7

— On my hon - ey - moon _____

I want to be where you

are. Dar - ling, can't you see

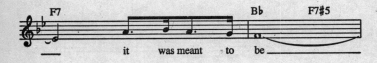

it was meant to be

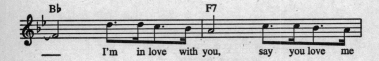

I'm in love with you, say you love me

too, sen - ti - men - tal me.

Sen - ti - men - tal me.

ROSETTA

Words and Music by EARL HINES
and HENRI WOOD

Ro - set - ta, _____ my Ro - set - ta, _____
told me, _____ that you love me, _____

_____ in my heart, dear, there's no one but you. _____
_____ nev - er leave me for

You some-bod - y new.

You've made my whole life a dream; _____

I pray you'll make it come true. _____ Ro -

set - ta, _____ my Ro - set - ta, _____ please say

I'm just the one dear for you. _____

SEPTEMBER SONG
from the Musical Play KNICKERBOCKER HOLIDAY
Words by MAXWELL ANDERSON
Music by KURT WEILL

SHOO FLY PIE AND APPLE PAN DOWDY

Lyric by SAMMY GALLOP
Music by GUY WOOD

Slow bounce - solid beat

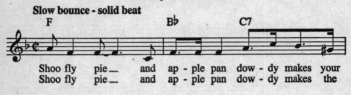

Shoo fly pie ___ and ap - ple pan dow - dy makes your
Shoo fly pie ___ and ap - ple pan dow - dy makes the

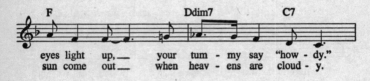

eyes light up, ___ your tum - my say "how - dy."
sun come out ___ when heav - ens are cloud - y.

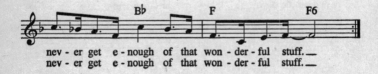

Shoo fly pie ___ and ap - ple pan dow - dy, ___ I
Shoo fly pie ___ and ap - ple pan dow - dy, ___ I

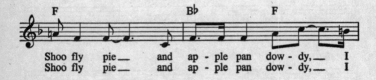

nev - er get e - nough of that won - der - ful stuff. ___
nev - er get e - nough of that won - der - ful stuff. ___

Ma - ma! when you bake, ___

Ma - ma! I don't want cake;

Ma - ma! For my sake___

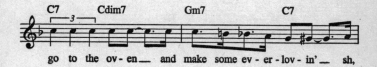

go to the ov - en___ and make some ev - er - lov - in'___ sh,

shoo fly pie___ and ap - ple pan dow - dy makes your

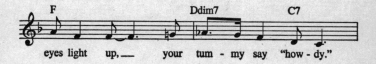

eyes light up, ___ your tum - my say "how - dy."

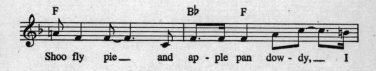

Shoo fly pie___ and ap - ple pan dow - dy, ___ I

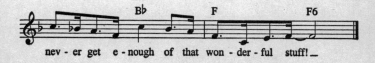

nev - er get e - nough of that won - der - ful stuff!___

SKYLARK

Words by JOHNNY MERCER
Music by HOAGY CARMICHAEL

Abmaj7 Db7 C7 Ddim7 C7
in the night. Won-der-ful mu-sic,
Fm7 Fdim7 Fm Eb7 Ab
faint as a "will-o' the wisp," craz-y as a loon,
G A7 D7 G Bb7
sad as a gyp-sy ser-e-nad-ing the moon. Oh,
Eb6 Bb7 Eb Ab
Sky-lark, I don't know if I can
Eb Gm Ab Eb
find these things. But my heart is rid-ing
Ab Eb F7 Bb7
on your wings, so, if you see them an-y-
Eb Bb7 Eb6
where won't you lead me there?

SLEEP WARM

**Words and Music by ALAN BERGMAN,
LEW SPENCE and MARILYN KEITH**

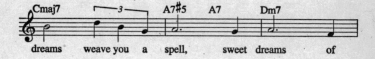

Sleep warm, sleep well, let

dreams weave you a spell, sweet dreams of

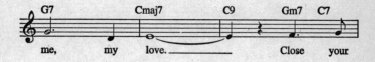

me, my love._____ Close your

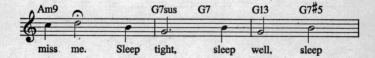

eyes now and kiss me and whis - per you'll

miss me. Sleep tight, sleep well, sleep

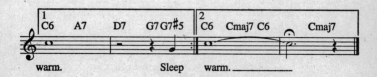

warm. Sleep warm._____

SOME DAY
(You'll Want Me To Want You)
Words and Music by
JIMMIE HODGES

Moderately

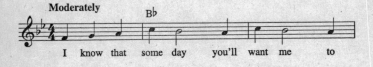

I know that some day you'll want me to

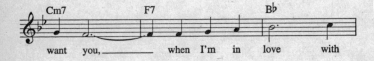

want you, _____ when I'm in love with

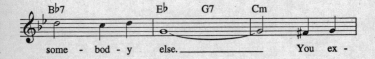

some - bod - y else. _____ You ex -

pect me to be true and keep on lov - ing

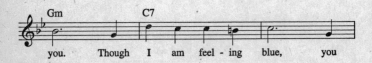

you. Though I am feel - ing blue, you

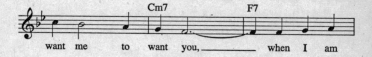

think I can't for - get you un - til some day you'll

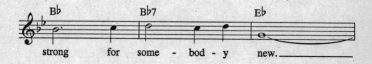

want me to want you, _____ when I am

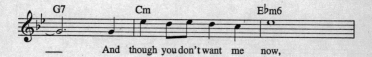

strong for some - bod - y new. _____

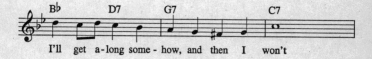

___ And though you don't want me now,

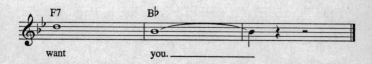

I'll get a - long some - how, and then I won't

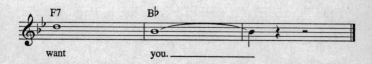

want you. _____

210 SOMEBODY LOVES YOU

Words by CHARLIE TOBIAS
Music by PETER DE ROSE

SPEAK LOW
from the Musical Production ONE TOUCH OF VENUS
Words by OGDEN NASH
Music by KURT WEILL

SPRING WILL BE A
LITTLE LATE THIS YEAR

from the Motion Picture CHRISTMAS HOLIDAY
By FRANK LOESSER

Moderately

Spring will be ___ a lit - tle late this

year, ___ a lit - tle late ar - riv - ing in

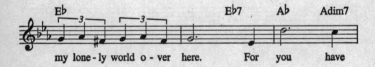

my lone - ly world o - ver here. For you have

left me, and where is our A - pril of old?

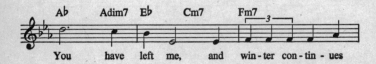

You have left me, and win - ter con - tin - ues

cold, as if to say spring will be ____ a lit - tle

slow to start, ____ a lit - tle slow re -

viv - ing that mu - sic it made in my heart. Yes,

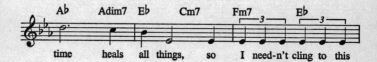

time heals all things, so I need - n't cling to this

fear, it's mere - ly that spring will be ____ a lit - tle

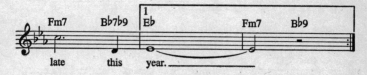

late this year. ____

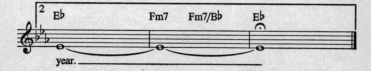

year. ____

SQUEEZE ME

Words and Music by CLARENCE WILLIAMS
and THOMAS "FATS" WALLER

F6 Ebmaj7 D7 G7 C7
gain oh, hon - ey, don't stop, 'til I tell you
F6 E7 F6 Eb7 D7 G7 C7
when. Now, ba - by, squeeze me and kiss me some
Fm Dm7b5 C/G G7
more, just like you did be -
Gm7 C7 F Eb7 D7 G7 C7
fore. Your ba - by cu - pid is stand - ing close
F6 Ebmaj7 D7 G7 C7
by, oh, {dad - dy / mom - ma} don't let your sweet ba - by
F9 F7 Bdim7 Bbdim7 Adim7 Abdim7 Gdim7
cry. Just pick me up
F#dim7 Fdim7 Edim7 Ebdim7 Ddim7 G7 Dm7 Gm7b5 G7
on your knee, I feel so good - y good - y when
1 C7 Gb7 F6 Eb7 D7
you kiss me. Oh, {dad - dy / mom - ma}
2 C7 Gb7 F6
you kiss me.

THE SURREY WITH THE FRINGE ON TOP

from OKLAHOMA!

Lyrics by OSCAR HAMMERSTEIN II
Music by RICHARD RODGERS

is - in - glass cur - tains, y' can roll right down, in

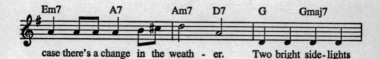

case there's a change in the weath - er. Two bright side - lights

wink - in' and blink - in', ain't no fin - er

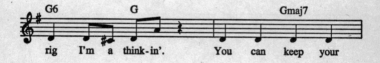

rig I'm a think - in'. You can keep your

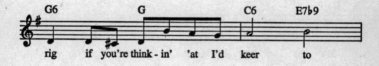

rig if you're think - in' 'at I'd keer to

swap fer that shin - y, lit - tle sur - rey with the

fringe on the top. _____

SWINGING ON A STAR

from GOING MY WAY

Words by JOHNNY BURKE
Music by JIMMY VAN HEUSEN

kicks up at an-y-thing he hears.____ His
shoes are a ter-ri-ble dis-grace.____ He's
can't write his name or read a book.____ To

back is brawn-y and his brain is weak,___ he's
got no man-ners when he eats his food,___ he's
fool the peo-ple is his on-ly thought,_ and

just plain stu-pid with a stub-born streak. And, by the
fat and la-zy and ex-treme-ly rude. But if you
though he's slip-per-y, he still gets caught. But then if

way, if you hate to go to school,
don't care a feath-er or a fig,
that sort of life is what you wish,

you may grow up to be a mule.____ Or would you
you may grow up to be a pig.____ Or would you
you may grow up to be a fish.____ And all the

222

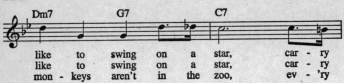

like   to   swing   on   a   star,   car - ry
like   to   swing   on   a   star,   car - ry
mon - keys   aren't   in   the   zoo,   ev - 'ry

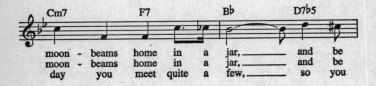

moon - beams   home   in   a   jar,_____   and   be
moon - beams   home   in   a   jar,_____   and   be
day   you   meet   quite   a   few,_____   so   you

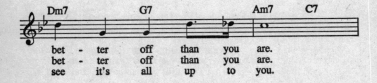

bet - ter   off   than   you   are.
bet - ter   off   than   you   are.
see   it's   all   up   to   you.

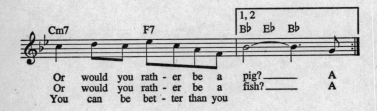

Or   would   you   rath - er   be   a   pig?____   A
Or   would   you   rath - er   be   a   fish?____   A
You   can   be   bet - ter   than   you

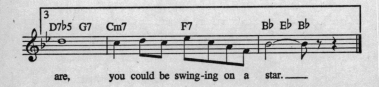

are,   you   could   be   swing-ing   on   a   star.____

SOFT LIGHTS AND SWEET MUSIC

from the Stage Production FACE THE MUSIC
Words and Music by
IRVING BERLIN

TENDERLY
from TORCH SONG
Lyric by JACK LAWRENCE
Music by WALTER GROSS

Moderately

The eve-ning breeze ca-ressed the trees ten - der -

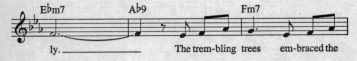

ly. _____ The trem-bling trees em-braced the

breeze ten - der - ly. _____ Then

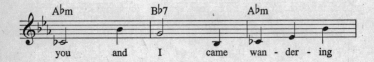

you and I came wan - der - ing

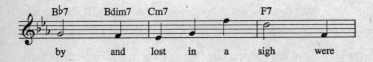

by and lost in a sigh were

225

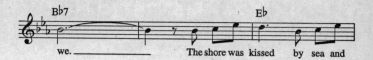

we._____ The shore was kissed by sea and

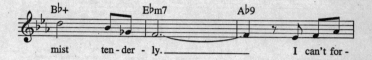

mist ten - der - ly._____ I can't for -

get how two hearts met breath-less - ly._____

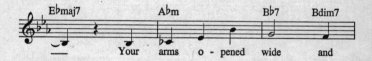

— Your arms o - pened wide and

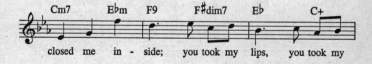

closed me in - side; you took my lips, you took my

love so ten - der - ly._____

THANKS FOR THE MEMORY

from the Paramount Picture BIG BROADCAST OF 1938

Words and Music by LEO ROBIN
and RALPH RAINGER

Thanks for the mem-o-ry of can-dle-light and wine,
cas-tles on the Rhine, the Par-the-non and mo-ments on the
Hud-son Riv-er Line. How love-ly it was!

Thanks for the mem-o-ry of rain-y af-ter-noons,
swing-y Har-lem tunes, and mo-tor trips and burn-ing lips and
burn-ing toast and prunes. How love-ly it was!

Thanks for the mem-o-ry of sen-ti-men-tal verse,
noth-ing in my purse, and chuck-les when the preach-er said, "For
bet-ter or for worse.". How love-ly it was!

Thanks for the mem-o-ry of lin-ge-rie with lace,
Pils-ner by the case, and how I jumped the day you trumped my
one and on-ly ace. How love-ly it was!

Man-y's the time that we feast-ed and
We said good-bye with a high-ball; then

THERE IS NO GREATER LOVE

Words by MARTY SYMES
Music by ISHAM JONES

With emotion

There is no great-er love than what I feel for

you, no great-er love,

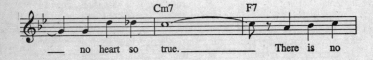

no heart so true. There is no

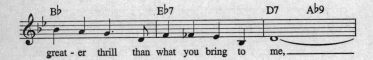

great-er thrill than what you bring to me,

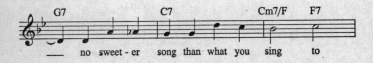

no sweet-er song than what you sing to

229

me.____ You're the sweet - est

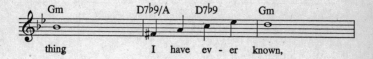
thing I have ev - er known,

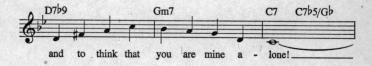
and to think that you are mine a - lone!____

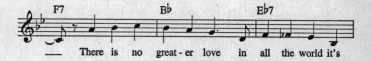
____ There is no great - er love in all the world it's

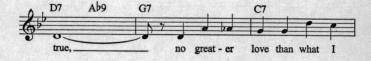
true,____ no great - er love than what I

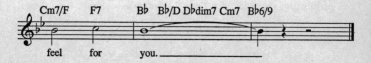
feel for you.____

THERE'S NO YOU

Words and Music by TOM ADAIR
and HAL HOPPER

Expressively

I feel _____ the au-tumn breeze. It
lone - ly au-tumn trees, how

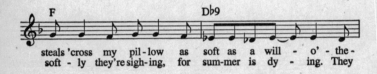

steals 'cross my pil-low as soft as a will - o' - the-
soft - ly they're sigh-ing, for sum-mer is dy - ing. They

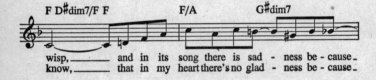

wisp, _____ and in its song there is sad - ness be-cause ___
know, _____ that in my heart there's no glad - ness be-cause ___

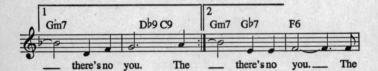

1
___ there's no you. The

2
___ there's no you. ___ The

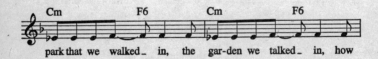

park that we walked _ in, the gar-den we talked _ in, how

lone-some they seem__ in the fall._____ The
storm-y clouds hov - er, and fall-ing leaves cov - er our
fav - or - ite nook__ in the wall.__ In
spring,_____ we'll meet a - gain. We'll
kiss and re-cap-ture the sum-mer-time rap - ture we
knew._____ And from that day, nev - er - more__ will I say.
__ there's no you!_____

THESE FOOLISH THINGS
(Remind Me of You)

Words by HOLT MARVELL
Music by JACK STRACHEY

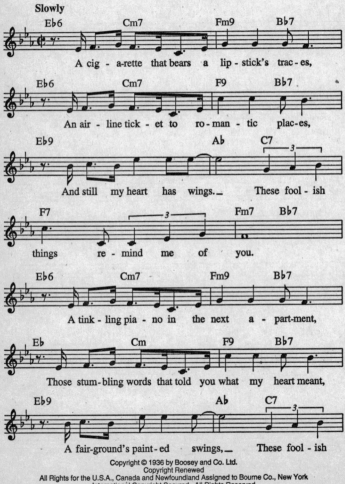

THEY SAY
IT'S WONDERFUL
from the Stage Production ANNIE GET YOUR GUN

Words and Music by
IRVING BERLIN

Bb   Bbm   F/A

can't re - call who said it,   I know I nev - er
leave your house some morn - ing,   and with - out an - y

Am

read it.   I   on - ly know they
warn - ing,   you're stop - ping peo - ple

G#dim   E7   Am   Abm6

tell me that love is grand,   and
shout - ing that love is grand.   And

Gm7   Bbm6/Db   C7

the thing that's known as ro - mance is
to hold a man in your arms is

Am7   D7#5(b9)   D7

won - der - ful,   won - der - ful
won - der - ful,   won - der - ful

G7sus   G9   Gm7   Gb7b5   [1] F6   Dm9

in ev - 'ry way, ___ so they say. ___
in ev - 'ry way, ___ *Annie:* so you

Gm9   F/A Abm6   [2] F6   Dm7   Gm7 Gb7 F6

___   say. ___

THIS LOVE OF MINE

Words and Music by SOL PARKER,
HENRY W. SANICOLA and FRANK SINATRA

Slowly

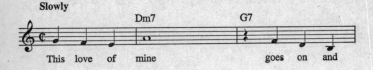

This love of mine goes on and

on, tho' life is emp - ty __

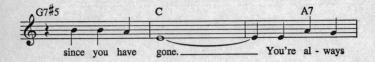

since you have gone. __ You're al - ways

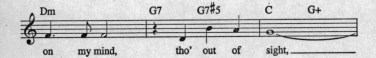

on my mind, tho' out of sight, __

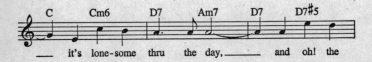

__ it's lone - some thru the day, __ and oh! the

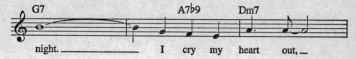

night._____ I cry my heart out,__

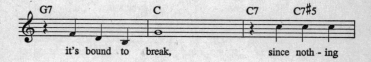

it's bound to break, since noth - ing

mat - ters__ let it break._____

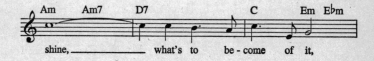

__ I ask the sun__ and the moon, the stars that

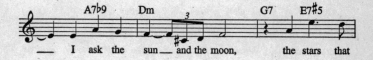

shine,_____ what's to be - come of it,

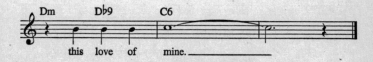

this love of mine._____

TIME AFTER TIME

from the Metro-Goldwyn-Mayer Picture IT HAPPENED IN BROOKLYN
Words by SAMMY CAHN
Music by JULE STYNE

YESTERDAYS

from ROBERTA
from LOVELY TO LOOK AT
Words by OTTO HARBACH
Music by JEROME KERN

TO LOVE AND BE LOVED
from the Film SOME CAME RUNNING
Words by SAMMY CAHN
Music by JAMES VAN HEUSEN

Moderately slow

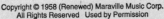

To love and be loved, that's what life's all a-bout,____

____ keeps the stars com-ing out. _____ What makes a

sad heart sing, the birds take wing? To love and be

loved, that's what liv-ing is for,_____ makes me

want you the more, the more we cling._____

____ Let oth - ers race to the moon____ through time and

WHY DO I LOVE YOU?

from SHOW BOAT

Lyrics by OSCAR HAMMERSTEIN II
Music by JEROME KERN

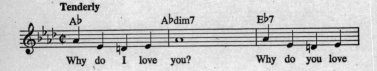

Why do I love you? Why do you love

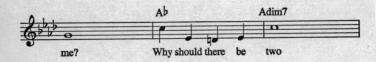

me? Why should there be two

hap - py as we?___ Can you see ___

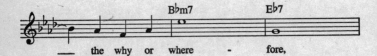

___ the why or where - fore,

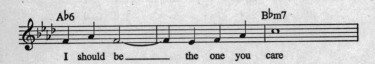

I should be ___ the one you care

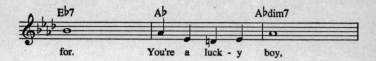

for.   You're a luck-y boy,

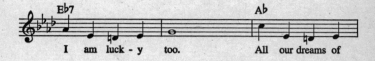

I am luck-y too.   All our dreams of

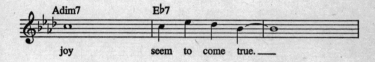

joy   seem to come true.___

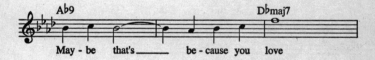

May-be that's___ be-cause you love

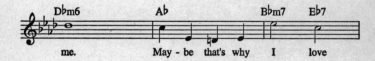

me.   May-be that's why I love

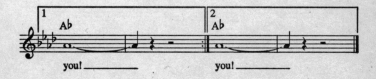

you!___   you!___

WILL YOU STILL BE MINE

Words by TOM ADAIR
Music by MATT DENNIS

WRAP YOUR TROUBLES IN DREAMS

(And Dream Your Troubles Away)

Lyric by TED KOEHLER and BILLY MOLL
Music by HARRY BARRIS

Moderately slow

When skies are cloud-y and gray, they're on-ly gray for a day, So wrap your trou-bles in dreams and dream your trou-bles a-way. Un-til that sun-shine peeps thru, there's on-ly one thing to do, just wrap your trou-bles in dreams and dream your trou-bles a-way. Your

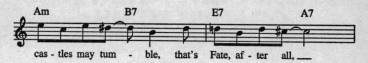

cas - tles may tum - ble, that's Fate, af - ter all, __

life's real - ly fun - ny that way.

No use to grum - ble, just smile as they fall, __

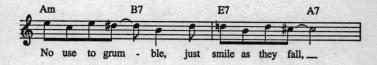

Were - n't you King __ for a day? Say!

Just re - mem-ber that sun - shine al - ways fol-lows the

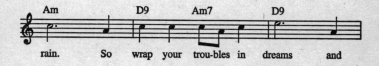

rain. So wrap your trou-bles in dreams and

dream your trou-bles a - way. When way.

YOU BROUGHT A NEW KIND OF LOVE TO ME

from the Paramount Picture THE BIG POND
from NEW YORK, NEW YORK

Words and Music by SAMMY FAIN,
IRVING KAHAL and PIERRE NORMAN

YOU DON'T KNOW
WHAT LOVE IS

Words and Music by DON RAYE
and GENE DePAUL

GUITAR CHORD FRAMES

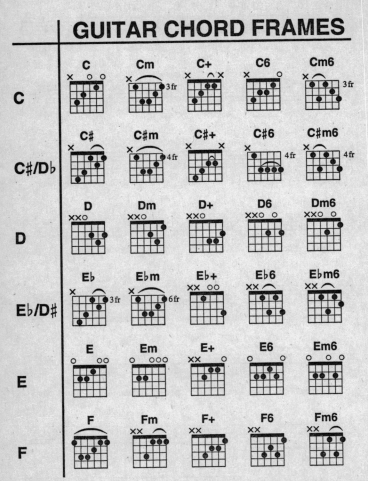

This guitar chord reference includes 120 commonly used chords. For a more complete guide to guitar chords, see "THE PAPERBACK CHORD BOOK" (HL00702009).

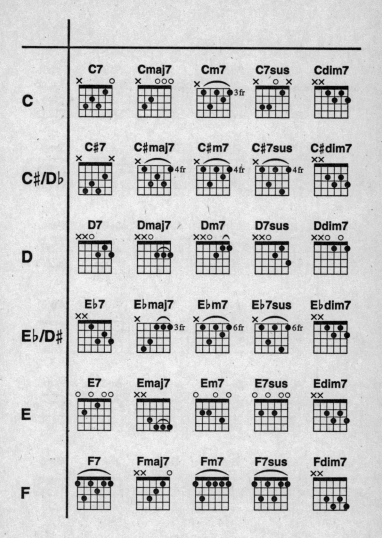

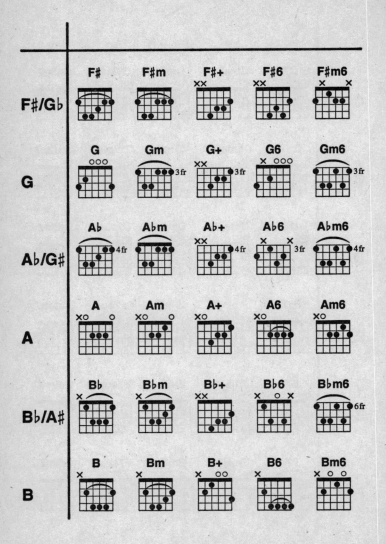